Cuisinart Bread Machine Cookbook

Delicious and Simple Recipes for Baking Artisan Bread at Home with Your Cuisinart Bread Maker

By

Monica D. Williams

Copyright©2024 Monica D. Williams
All rights reserved. No part of this book may be reproduced, stored in a retrieval system, or transmitted in any form or by any means—electronic, mechanical, photocopying, recording, or otherwise—without the prior written permission of the publisher, except for brief quotations in critical reviews or articles.

Table of Contents

INTRODUCTION

GETTING STARTED WITH YOUR CUISINART BREAD MACHINE

CHAPTER ONE

BASIC BREADS
CLASSIC WHITE BREAD
WHOLE WHEAT BREAD
MULTIGRAIN BREAD
FRENCH BAGUETTE
ITALIAN BREAD
RYE BREAD
OATMEAL HONEY BREAD
GRAIN BREAD
POTATO ROSEMARY BREAD
SUNFLOWER SEED BREAD
CINNAMON SWIRL BREAD
HONEY WHEAT BREAD
CRANBERRY WALNUT BREAD
PARMESAN HERB BREAD

CHAPTER TWO

SWEET BREADS
CINNAMON SWIRL RAISIN BREAD
CHOCOLATE CHIP BANANA BREAD
CRANBERRY ORANGE NUT BREAD
LEMON POPPY SEED BREAD
APPLE CINNAMON BREAD
PUMPKIN SPICE BREAD
CHERRY ALMOND BREAD
BLUEBERRY LEMON BREAD
PECAN MAPLE BREAD
NUTELLA SWIRL BREAD
RASPBERRY ALMOND BREAD
APRICOT WALNUT BREAD

CHAPTER THREE

SPECIALTY BREADS
Rosemary Garlic Focaccia
Olive and Herb Ciabatta
Sun-Dried Tomato and Parmesan Bread
Cranberry Pecan Bread
Cheddar Jalapeño Bread
Fig and Walnut Bread
Pesto and Sun-Dried Tomato Bread
Maple Bacon Bread
Caramelized Onion and Gruyère Bread
Multigrain Seeded Bread
Herb and Cheese Fougasse
Sourdough Rye Bread
Garlic and Herb Knots
Chocolate Cherry Brioche
Prosciutto and Parmesan Focaccia

CHAPTER FOUR

GLUTEN-FREE BREADS
Classic Gluten-Free White Bread
Chia Seed and Quinoa Bread
Almond Flour Banana Bread
Sweet Potato and Walnut Bread
Spinach and Feta Socca Bread
Hazelnut and Fig Bread
Cranberry Orange Quinoa Bread
Rosemary Parmesan Chickpea Bread
Pumpkin Seed and Teff Bread
Coconut Flour Banana Bread
Sorghum and Seed Bread
Raspberry Almond Flour Bread
Millet and Sun-Dried Tomato Bread
Pistachio and Cranberry Bread
Buckwheat and Date Bread

CHAPTER FIVE

ARTISAN BREADS

Classic French Baguette
Italian Ciabatta
Sourdough Artisan Boule
Whole Grain Seeded Bread
Rosemary and Olive No-Knead Bread
Cranberry Walnut Artisan Bread
Rustic Rye Bread
Sun-Dried Tomato and Basil Fougasse
Herb and Cheese Swirl Bread
Multigrain Harvest Loaf
Walnut and Fig Artisan Bread
Caramelized Onion and Gruyere Fougasse
Cranberry Pecan Sourdough Bread
Garlic and Herb Focaccia
Challah Bread with Sesame Seeds

CHAPTER SIX

Holiday and Special Occasion Breads
Cranberry Orange Walnut Bread
Chocolate Pecan Swirl Bread
Maple Pecan Pumpkin Bread
Rosemary and Cranberry Focaccia
Chocolate Cherry Bread
Almond and Orange Twist Bread
Pumpkin Spice Cinnamon Swirl Bread
Holiday Nutmeg Eggnog Bread
Caramel Pecan Monkey Bread
Gingerbread Loaf with Cream Cheese Swirl
Cherry Almond Brioche Wreath
Orange Cranberry Babka
Cinnamon Roll Swirl Bread with Cream Cheese Glaze
Chocolate Orange Braided Bread
Hazelnut Praline Twist Bread

CHAPTER SEVEN

Jam and Nut Dispenser Recipes
Strawberry Almond Jam Swirl Bread
Apricot Walnut Dispenser Bread
Raspberry Hazelnut Swirl Loaf

Blueberry Pecan Burst Bread
Cherry Chocolate Nut Delight
Raspberry Almond Crunch Bread
Blackberry Walnut Surprise Loaf
Apple Cinnamon Pecan Delight Bread
Fig and Pistachio Swirl Bread
Cranberry Orange Walnut Bliss
Mango Coconut Macadamia Bread
Pomegranate Pistachio Delight
Pear Ginger Walnut Swirl Bread
Cherry Pistachio Coconut Loaf

CHAPTER EIGHT

Dough-Only Recipes
Classic Pizza Dough
Soft Pretzel Dough
Garlic Herb Breadsticks Dough
Cinnamon Roll Dough
Herb Focaccia Dough
Bagel Dough
Whole Wheat Bread Dough
Pita Bread Dough
Brioche Dough
Olive and Rosemary Fougasse Dough
Sourdough Bread Dough
Sun-Dried Tomato and Basil Bread Dough
Cranberry Walnut Bread Dough
Pesto Swirl Bread Dough
Chocolate Babka Dough
Honey Oat Bread Dough

CHAPTER NINE

Troubleshooting and Tips

CONCLUSION

Introduction

Welcome to the world of homemade bread baking with your Cuisinart Bread Machine! This cookbook is intended to be your reliable companion on a wonderful journey into the art of making delicious and nutritious bread in the comfort of your own kitchen.

These pages contain a range of delicious dishes that cater to a variety of tastes and preferences. From the simplicity of conventional white bread to the complexity of gourmet sourdough, we've compiled a broad collection of recipes to fit every occasion or craving.

Getting Started With Your Cuisinart Bread Machine

Congratulations on your new Cuisinart bread machine! Whether you're a rookie baker or a seasoned pro, this multipurpose kitchen device is designed to make bread-making simple. With the capacity to mix, knead, rise, and bake bread all in one gadget, you're about to begin on a delicious adventure of making homemade breads that are not only rewarding to produce but also pleasant to eat. Here's everything you should know to get started.

Unboxing and Initial Setup

- Read the manual. Before you do anything, read the handbook. It includes important information about your particular model, such as safety precautions, part specifications, and warranty information.
- Inspect your machine to ensure all parts are intact and undamaged. Your Cuisinart Bread Machine should have a baking pan, kneading paddle(s), and a measuring cup and spoon.
- Clean the baking pan and kneading paddle with warm soapy water. Wipe off the machine's interior and exterior with a moist cloth. Before reassembling, make sure to completely dry all parts.
- Find the Best Location: Place your bread machine on a sturdy, level platform away from water and heat. Make sure there is enough clearance around the appliance for air circulation.

Understanding Your Bread Machine

- Control panel: Familiarize yourself with the controls. Learn how to adjust various variables, such as bread type, crust color, and loaf size, based on your model.
- Cuisinart Bread Machines provide programs for many bread kinds, including white, whole wheat, French, gluten-free, and jams/cakes. Experiment with these options until you find your favorites.
- Some versions include a delay start timer, allowing you to add ingredients and prepare fresh bread later. Ideal for waking up to the smell of freshly made bread!

Your First Loaf

1. Begin with a simple recipe, like white bread, to acquire a sense of the process. Your machine's manual is likely to feature a few recipes tailored exclusively for your model.
2. Measure ingredients precisely. Use the provided measuring cup and spoon to correctly measure your ingredients. Your bread's success is greatly dependent on the amounts of ingredients.
3. Follow the recommended order of adding ingredients: liquids first, then dry. Yeast should be added last, so that it does not come into touch with the liquid until the machine starts mixing.
4. Select the appropriate program for your recipe, including bread type, crust color, and loaf size. Then simply click the start button and let your Cuisinart Bread Machine handle the rest.
5. Cooling: After baking, remove the bread pan with oven mitts. Transfer the bread to a wire rack and let it cool before slicing. This keeps the bread from getting soggy.

Tips for Success

- Experiment: Don't be scared to explore new recipes and settings. Each batch of bread represents an opportunity to learn and improve your skills.
- Refer to your manual's troubleshooting section if your bread fails to meet expectations. Common problems are generally solved with easy changes like as changing ingredient amounts or ensuring that the yeast is fresh.
- Maintenance: Keep your bread maker clean and functional. Regularly inspect the kneading paddle and bread pan for wear and tear.

Starting with your Cuisinart Bread Machine provides up a plethora of culinary options. From classic loaves to artisanal breads and beyond, you may experience the delight of preparing fresh, handcrafted bread.

Chapter One

Basic Breads

Classic White Bread

Prep Time: 10 minutes
Cook Time: 3 hours
Serving Size: 12 slices

Ingredients:

- 1 1/2 cups warm water
- 2 tablespoons sugar
- 1 1/2 teaspoons salt
- 4 cups bread flour
- 2 tablespoons unsalted butter, softened
- 2 teaspoons active dry yeast

Instructions:

1. Place all ingredients in the bread machine in the order recommended by the manufacturer.
2. Select the basic white bread setting and press start.
3. Allow the bread machine to complete the cycle.
4. Once done, let the bread cool before slicing.

Nutritional Value (per slice):

- Calories: 120
- Protein: 3g
- Carbohydrates: 21g
- Fat: 2g

- Fiber: 1g

Whole Wheat Bread

Prep Time: 15 minutes
Cook Time: 3 hours 30 minutes
Serving Size: 14 slices

Ingredients:

- 1 1/4 cups warm water
- 2 tablespoons honey
- 1 1/2 teaspoons salt
- 2 cups whole wheat flour
- 2 cups bread flour
- 2 tablespoons olive oil
- 2 teaspoons active dry yeast

Instructions:

1. Add ingredients to the bread machine following the manufacturer's guidelines.
2. Choose the whole wheat setting and start the machine.
3. Allow the bread to cool for a few minutes before slicing.

Nutritional Value (per slice):

- Calories: 110
- Protein: 3.5g
- Carbohydrates: 20g
- Fat: 2g
- Fiber: 3g

Multigrain Bread

Prep Time: 20 minutes
Cook Time: 3 hours 15 minutes
Serving Size: 16 slices

Ingredients:

- 1 1/3 cups warm milk
- 2 tablespoons honey
- 1 1/2 teaspoons salt
- 1 cup bread flour
- 1 cup whole wheat flour
- 1/2 cup oats
- 1/4 cup flaxseeds
- 2 teaspoons active dry yeast

Instructions:

1. Place ingredients into the bread machine as per the manufacturer's instructions.
2. Choose the multigrain setting and start the machine.
3. Once done, allow the bread to cool before slicing.

Nutritional Value (per slice):

- Calories: 95
- Protein: 3g
- Carbohydrates: 17g
- Fat: 2g
- Fiber: 2.5g

French Baguette

Prep Time: 20 minutes
Cook Time: 2 hours 30 minutes
Serving Size: 2 baguettes (12 slices each)

Ingredients:

- 1 1/4 cups warm water
- 1 teaspoon sugar
- 1 1/2 teaspoons salt
- 3 1/2 cups bread flour
- 1 1/2 teaspoons active dry yeast

Instructions:

1. Add ingredients to the bread machine following the manufacturer's guidelines.
2. Select the French bread setting and press start.
3. Allow the machine to complete the cycle, then cool the baguettes on a wire rack before slicing.

Nutritional Value (per slice):

- Calories: 90
- Protein: 2.5g
- Carbohydrates: 18g
- Fat: 0.5g
- Fiber: 1g

Italian Bread

Prep Time: 15 minutes
Cook Time: 3 hours
Serving Size: 10 slices

Ingredients:

- 1 1/3 cups warm water
- 1 tablespoon sugar
- 1 1/2 teaspoons salt
- 3 1/4 cups bread flour
- 2 tablespoons olive oil
- 2 teaspoons active dry yeast

Instructions:

1. Place ingredients into the bread machine according to the manufacturer's instructions.
2. Choose the Italian bread setting and start the machine.
3. Once baked, cool the Italian bread before slicing.

Nutritional Value (per slice):

- Calories: 120
- Protein: 3g
- Carbohydrates: 21g
- Fat: 2.5g
- Fiber: 1g

Rye Bread

Prep Time: 15 minutes
Cook Time: 3 hours 15 minutes
Serving Size: 12 slices

Ingredients:

- 1 1/4 cups warm water
- 2 tablespoons molasses
- 1 1/2 teaspoons salt
- 1 1/2 cups bread flour
- 1 cup rye flour
- 1 tablespoon caraway seeds
- 2 teaspoons active dry yeast

Instructions:

1. Add ingredients to the bread machine following the manufacturer's guidelines.
2. Choose the rye bread setting and start the machine.
3. Allow the bread to cool before slicing.

Nutritional Value (per slice):

- Calories: 100
- Protein: 2.5g
- Carbohydrates: 21g
- Fat: 0.5g
- Fiber: 2g

Oatmeal Honey Bread

Prep Time: 15 minutes
Cook Time: 3 hours
Serving Size: 14 slices

Ingredients:

- 1 1/4 cups warm milk
- 2 tablespoons honey
- 1 1/2 teaspoons salt
- 1 cup rolled oats
- 3 cups bread flour
- 2 teaspoons active dry yeast

Instructions:

1. Place ingredients into the bread machine as per the manufacturer's instructions.
2. Choose the basic bread setting with medium crust and start the machine.
3. Once baked, cool the oatmeal honey bread on a wire rack before slicing.

Nutritional Value (per slice):

- Calories: 110
- Protein: 3g
- Carbohydrates: 20g
- Fat: 2g
- Fiber: 2.5g

Grain Bread

Prep Time: 20 minutes
Cook Time: 3 hours 30 minutes
Serving Size: 16 slices

Ingredients:

- 1 1/3 cups warm water
- 2 tablespoons honey
- 1 1/2 teaspoons salt
- 1 cup bread flour
- 1/2 cup whole wheat flour
- 1/4 cup each of 5 additional grains (quinoa, amaranth, millet, buckwheat, barley)
- 2 teaspoons active dry yeast

Instructions:

1. Add ingredients to the bread machine following the manufacturer's guidelines.
2. Choose the whole grain setting and start the machine.
3. Allow the bread to cool for a few minutes before slicing.

Nutritional Value (per slice):

- Calories: 95
- Protein: 3.5g
- Carbohydrates: 18g
- Fat: 2g
- Fiber: 3g

Potato Rosemary Bread

Prep Time: 15 minutes
Cook Time: 3 hours
Serving Size: 12 slices

Ingredients:

- 1 cup warm mashed potatoes
- 1 1/2 teaspoons salt
- 3 1/2 cups bread flour
- 2 tablespoons olive oil
- 2 teaspoons dried rosemary
- 2 teaspoons active dry yeast

Instructions:

1. Place ingredients into the bread machine as per the manufacturer's instructions.
2. Choose the basic bread setting and start the machine.
3. Once baked, cool the potato rosemary bread on a wire rack before slicing.

Nutritional Value (per slice):

- Calories: 130
- Protein: 3g
- Carbohydrates: 24g
- Fat: 2.5g

Sunflower Seed Bread

Prep Time: 15 minutes
Cook Time: 3 hours 15 minutes
Serving Size: 14 slices

Ingredients:

- 1 1/3 cups warm water
- 2 tablespoons honey
- 1 1/2 teaspoons salt
- 3 cups bread flour
- 1/2 cup sunflower seeds
- 2 tablespoons olive oil
- 2 teaspoons active dry yeast

Instructions:

1. Add ingredients to the bread machine following the manufacturer's guidelines.
2. Choose the whole grain setting and start the machine.
3. Allow the bread to cool before slicing.

Nutritional Value (per slice):

- Calories: 110
- Protein: 3g
- Carbohydrates: 19g
- Fat: 2.5g
- Fiber: 2g

Cornbread

Prep Time: 10 minutes
Cook Time: 2 hours
Serving Size: 12 slices

Ingredients:

- 1 cup cornmeal
- 1 cup all-purpose flour
- 2 teaspoons baking powder
- 1 teaspoon salt
- 2 tablespoons sugar
- 1 cup milk
- 2 tablespoons melted butter
- 2 teaspoons active dry yeast

Instructions:

1. Add dry ingredients to the bread machine, followed by the wet ingredients, and finally the yeast.
2. Select the quick bread or cake setting and start the machine.
3. Allow the cornbread to cool before slicing.

Nutritional Value (per slice):

- Calories: 130
- Protein: 3g
- Carbohydrates: 21g
- Fat: 4g
- Fiber: 2g

Cinnamon Swirl Bread

Prep Time: 20 minutes
Cook Time: 3 hours
Serving Size: 16 slices

Ingredients:

- 1 1/4 cups warm milk
- 2 tablespoons sugar
- 1 1/2 teaspoons salt
- 3 1/2 cups bread flour
- 2 tablespoons unsalted butter, softened
- 2 teaspoons ground cinnamon
- 1/4 cup brown sugar
- 2 teaspoons active dry yeast

Instructions:

1. Place ingredients into the bread machine as per the manufacturer's instructions.
2. Choose the sweet bread setting and start the machine.
3. Allow the cinnamon swirl bread to cool before slicing.

Nutritional Value (per slice):

- Calories: 120
- Protein: 3g
- Carbohydrates: 22g
- Fat: 2.5g
- Fiber: 1.5g

Honey Wheat Bread

Prep Time: 15 minutes
Cook Time: 3 hours
Serving Size: 14 slices

Ingredients:

- 1 1/3 cups warm water
- 2 tablespoons honey
- 1 1/2 teaspoons salt
- 2 cups whole wheat flour
- 1 1/2 cups bread flour
- 2 tablespoons olive oil
- 2 teaspoons active dry yeast

Instructions:

1. Add ingredients to the bread machine following the manufacturer's guidelines.
2. Choose the whole wheat setting and start the machine.
3. Allow the honey wheat bread to cool on a wire rack before slicing.

Nutritional Value (per slice):

- Calories: 110
- Protein: 3g
- Carbohydrates: 21g
- Fat: 2g
- Fiber: 3g

Cranberry Walnut Bread

Prep Time: 20 minutes
Cook Time: 3 hours
Serving Size: 12 slices

Ingredients:

- 1 1/4 cups warm water
- 2 tablespoons honey
- 1 1/2 teaspoons salt
- 3 cups bread flour
- 1/2 cup dried cranberries
- 1/2 cup chopped walnuts
- 2 teaspoons active dry yeast

Instructions:

1. Place ingredients into the bread machine as per the manufacturer's instructions.
2. Choose the basic bread setting with medium crust and start the machine.
3. Once baked, cool the cranberry walnut bread on a wire rack before slicing.

Nutritional Value (per slice):

- Calories: 130
- Protein: 3g
- Carbohydrates: 22g
- Fat: 3g
- Fiber: 2g

Parmesan Herb Bread

Prep Time: 15 minutes
Cook Time: 3 hours
Serving Size: 16 slices

Ingredients:

- 1 1/3 cups warm milk
- 2 tablespoons grated Parmesan cheese
- 1 1/2 teaspoons salt
- 4 cups bread flour
- 2 tablespoons chopped fresh herbs (rosemary, thyme, oregano)
- 2 teaspoons active dry yeast

Instructions:

1. Add ingredients to the bread machine following the manufacturer's guidelines.
2. Choose the basic bread setting with light crust and start the machine.
3. Allow the Parmesan herb bread to cool before slicing.

Nutritional Value (per slice):

- Calories: 120
- Protein: 3g
- Carbohydrates: 21g
- Fat: 2g
- Fiber: 1g

Chapter Two

Sweet Breads

Cinnamon Swirl Raisin Bread

Prep Time: 15 minutes
Cook Time: 3 hours
Serving Size: 12 slices

Ingredients:

- 1 cup warm milk
- 2 tablespoons unsalted butter, melted
- 1 1/2 teaspoons salt
- 3 cups bread flour
- 1/4 cup sugar
- 2 teaspoons ground cinnamon
- 1/2 cup raisins
- 2 teaspoons active dry yeast

Instructions:

1. Add ingredients to the bread machine following the manufacturer's guidelines.
2. Choose the sweet bread setting and start the machine.
3. Once baked, cool the cinnamon swirl raisin bread on a wire rack before slicing.

Nutritional Value (per slice):

- Calories: 130
- Protein: 3g
- Carbohydrates: 25g

- Fat: 2g
- Fiber: 1g

Chocolate Chip Banana Bread

Prep Time: 15 minutes
Cook Time: 3 hours
Serving Size: 12 slices

Ingredients:

- 3 ripe bananas, mashed
- 1/2 cup unsalted butter, melted
- 1 teaspoon vanilla extract
- 2 eggs
- 2 cups all-purpose flour
- 1 teaspoon baking soda
- 1/4 teaspoon salt
- 1/2 cup chocolate chips
- 2 teaspoons active dry yeast

Instructions:

1. Place wet ingredients in the bread machine, followed by dry ingredients, and finally the yeast.
2. Choose the sweet bread setting and start the machine.
3. Allow the chocolate chip banana bread to cool before slicing.

Nutritional Value (per slice):

- Calories: 180

- Protein: 3g
- Carbohydrates: 24g
- Fat: 8g
- Fiber: 2g

Cranberry Orange Nut Bread

Prep Time: 20 minutes
Cook Time: 3 hours
Serving Size: 14 slices

Ingredients:

- 1 cup orange juice
- 1/4 cup vegetable oil
- 1 teaspoon vanilla extract
- 2 eggs
- 3 cups bread flour
- 1/2 cup sugar
- 1 1/2 teaspoons baking powder
- 1/2 teaspoon salt
- 1 cup dried cranberries
- 1/2 cup chopped nuts (walnuts or pecans)
- 2 teaspoons active dry yeast

Instructions:

1. Add ingredients to the bread machine following the manufacturer's guidelines.
2. Choose the sweet bread setting with light crust and start the machine.

3. Once baked, cool the cranberry orange nut bread on a wire rack before slicing.

Nutritional Value (per slice):

- Calories: 150
- Protein: 3g
- Carbohydrates: 26g
- Fat: 4g
- Fiber: 1.5g

Lemon Poppy Seed Bread

Prep Time: 15 minutes
Cook Time: 3 hours
Serving Size: 12 slices

Ingredients:

- 1 cup warm milk
- 1/4 cup vegetable oil
- 1 teaspoon vanilla extract
- Zest of 1 lemon
- 2 tablespoons fresh lemon juice
- 2 eggs
- 3 cups bread flour
- 1/2 cup sugar
- 1 tablespoon poppy seeds
- 2 teaspoons active dry yeast

Instructions:

1. Place wet ingredients in the bread machine, followed by dry ingredients, and finally the yeast.
2. Choose the sweet bread setting with medium crust and start the machine.
3. Once baked, cool the lemon poppy seed bread on a wire rack before slicing.

Nutritional Value (per slice):

- Calories: 140
- Protein: 3g
- Carbohydrates: 24g
- Fat: 3g
- Fiber: 1g

Apple Cinnamon Bread

Prep Time: 20 minutes
Cook Time: 3 hours
Serving Size: 14 slices

Ingredients:

- 2 cups peeled and finely chopped apples
- 1/4 cup unsalted butter, melted
- 1 teaspoon vanilla extract
- 2 eggs
- 3 cups bread flour
- 1/2 cup sugar
- 1 teaspoon ground cinnamon
- 1/2 teaspoon nutmeg

- 1/2 teaspoon salt
- 1 cup chopped pecans or walnuts (optional)
- 2 teaspoons active dry yeast

Instructions:

1. Add ingredients to the bread machine following the manufacturer's guidelines.
2. Choose the sweet bread setting and start the machine.
3. Allow the apple cinnamon bread to cool before slicing.

Nutritional Value (per slice):

- Calories: 160
- Protein: 3g
- Carbohydrates: 24g
- Fat: 6g
- Fiber: 2g

Pumpkin Spice Bread

Prep Time: 15 minutes
Cook Time: 3 hours
Serving Size: 16 slices

Ingredients:

- 1 cup canned pumpkin puree
- 1/4 cup vegetable oil
- 1 teaspoon vanilla extract
- 2 eggs
- 3 cups bread flour

- 1/2 cup brown sugar
- 1 teaspoon ground cinnamon
- 1/2 teaspoon ground ginger
- 1/4 teaspoon ground nutmeg
- 1/4 teaspoon ground cloves
- 2 teaspoons active dry yeast

Instructions:

1. Place wet ingredients in the bread machine, followed by dry ingredients, and finally the yeast.
2. Choose the sweet bread setting with light crust and start the machine.
3. Once baked, cool the pumpkin spice bread on a wire rack before slicing.

Nutritional Value (per slice):

- Calories: 130
- Protein: 3g
- Carbohydrates: 23g
- Fat: 3g
- Fiber: 1.5g

Cherry Almond Bread

Prep Time: 20 minutes
Cook Time: 3 hours
Serving Size: 12 slices

Ingredients:

- 1 cup warm milk

- 1/4 cup unsalted butter, softened
- 1 teaspoon almond extract
- 2 eggs
- 3 cups bread flour
- 1/2 cup sugar
- 1/2 teaspoon salt
- 1 cup dried cherries
- 1/2 cup chopped almonds
- 2 teaspoons active dry yeast

Instructions:

1. Add ingredients to the bread machine following the manufacturer's guidelines.
2. Choose the sweet bread setting and start the machine.
3. Once baked, cool the cherry almond bread on a wire rack before slicing.

Nutritional Value (per slice):

- Calories: 160
- Protein: 4g
- Carbohydrates: 26g
- Fat: 4g
- Fiber: 2g

Blueberry Lemon Bread

Prep Time: 15 minutes
Cook Time: 3 hours
Serving Size: 14 slices

Ingredients:

- 1 cup fresh or frozen blueberries
- 1/4 cup unsalted butter, melted
- 1 teaspoon lemon zest
- 2 tablespoons fresh lemon juice
- 2 eggs
- 3 cups bread flour
- 1/2 cup sugar
- 1/2 teaspoon salt
- 1/2 teaspoon baking powder
- 2 teaspoons active dry yeast

Instructions:

1. Add ingredients to the bread machine following the manufacturer's guidelines.
2. Choose the sweet bread setting with light crust and start the machine.
3. Allow the blueberry lemon bread to cool before slicing.

Nutritional Value (per slice):

- Calories: 140
- Protein: 3g
- Carbohydrates: 26g
- Fat: 3g

- Fiber: 2g

Pecan Maple Bread

Prep Time: 15 minutes
Cook Time: 3 hours
Serving Size: 16 slices

Ingredients:

- 1 1/4 cups warm milk
- 2 tablespoons maple syrup
- 1/4 cup unsalted butter, melted
- 1/2 cup chopped pecans
- 2 eggs
- 3 cups bread flour
- 1/2 cup sugar
- 1/2 teaspoon salt
- 2 teaspoons active dry yeast

Instructions:

1. Place ingredients into the bread machine as per the manufacturer's instructions.
2. Choose the sweet bread setting and start the machine.
3. Once baked, cool the pecan maple bread on a wire rack before slicing.

Nutritional Value (per slice):

- Calories: 150
- Protein: 3.5g
- Carbohydrates: 24g
- Fat: 4g

- Fiber: 1.5g

Nutella Swirl Bread

Prep Time: 15 minutes
Cook Time: 3 hours
Serving Size: 12 slices

Ingredients:

- 1 cup warm milk
- 1/4 cup unsalted butter, softened
- 1/2 cup Nutella
- 2 eggs
- 3 cups bread flour
- 1/4 cup sugar
- 1/2 teaspoon salt
- 2 teaspoons active dry yeast

Instructions:

1. Add ingredients to the bread machine following the manufacturer's guidelines.
2. Choose the sweet bread setting and start the machine.
3. Once the dough is ready, roll it out, spread Nutella evenly, roll it back into a loaf, and place it in the bread machine.
4. Continue baking according to the machine's instructions.
5. Allow the Nutella swirl bread to cool before slicing.

Nutritional Value (per slice):

- Calories: 180
- Protein: 4g

- Carbohydrates: 26g
- Fat: 7g
- Fiber: 1g

Raspberry Almond Bread

Prep Time: 20 minutes
Cook Time: 3 hours
Serving Size: 14 slices

Ingredients:

- 1 cup warm milk
- 1/4 cup unsalted butter, melted
- 1 teaspoon almond extract
- 2 eggs
- 3 cups bread flour
- 1/2 cup sugar
- 1/2 teaspoon salt
- 1 cup fresh or frozen raspberries
- 1/2 cup sliced almonds
- 2 teaspoons active dry yeast

Instructions:

1. Add ingredients to the bread machine following the manufacturer's guidelines.
2. Choose the sweet bread setting and start the machine.
3. Gently fold in raspberries and almonds once the machine signals the addition of mix-ins.

4. Allow the raspberry almond bread to cool before slicing.

Nutritional Value (per slice):

- Calories: 150
- Protein: 4g
- Carbohydrates: 25g
- Fat: 4g
- Fiber: 2g

Apricot Walnut Bread

Prep Time: 15 minutes
Cook Time: 3 hours
Serving Size: 16 slices

Ingredients:

- 1 1/4 cups warm milk
- 2 tablespoons honey
- 1/4 cup unsalted butter, softened
- 1/2 cup dried apricots, chopped
- 1/2 cup chopped walnuts
- 2 eggs
- 3 cups bread flour
- 1/4 cup sugar
- 1/2 teaspoon salt
- 2 teaspoons active dry yeast

Instructions:

1. Add ingredients to the bread machine following the manufacturer's guidelines.
2. Choose the sweet bread setting and start the machine.
3. Gently fold in apricots and walnuts once the machine signals the addition of mix-ins.
4. Allow the apricot walnut bread to cool before slicing.

Nutritional Value (per slice):

- Calories: 140
- Protein: 4g
- Carbohydrates: 24g
- Fat: 3.5g
- Fiber: 2g

Chapter Three

Specialty Breads

Rosemary Garlic Focaccia

Prep Time: 20 minutes
Cook Time: 3 hours
Serving Size: 12 slices

Ingredients:

- 1 1/4 cups warm water
- 2 tablespoons olive oil
- 1 1/2 teaspoons salt
- 3 1/2 cups bread flour
- 1 tablespoon sugar
- 2 teaspoons dried rosemary
- 2 cloves garlic, minced
- 2 teaspoons active dry yeast

Instructions:

1. Add ingredients to the bread machine following the manufacturer's guidelines.
2. Choose the focaccia setting and start the machine.
3. Once baked, cool the focaccia on a wire rack before slicing.

Nutritional Value (per slice):

- Calories: 120
- Protein: 3g
- Carbohydrates: 21g

- Fat: 2.5g
- Fiber: 1g

Olive and Herb Ciabatta

Prep Time: 25 minutes
Cook Time: 3 hours
Serving Size: 16 slices

Ingredients:

- 1 1/3 cups warm water
- 2 tablespoons olive oil
- 1 1/2 teaspoons salt
- 3 1/2 cups bread flour
- 1/2 cup pitted and chopped mixed olives
- 2 teaspoons dried basil
- 1 teaspoon dried oregano
- 2 teaspoons active dry yeast

Instructions:

1. Add ingredients to the bread machine following the manufacturer's guidelines.
2. Choose the ciabatta setting and start the machine.
3. Once baked, cool the ciabatta on a wire rack before slicing.

Nutritional Value (per slice):

- Calories: 110
- Protein: 3g
- Carbohydrates: 20g

- Fat: 2g
- Fiber: 1.5g

Sun-Dried Tomato and Parmesan Bread

Prep Time: 15 minutes
Cook Time: 3 hours
Serving Size: 14 slices

Ingredients:

- 1 1/4 cups warm water
- 2 tablespoons olive oil
- 1 1/2 teaspoons salt
- 3 1/4 cups bread flour
- 1/2 cup sun-dried tomatoes, chopped
- 1/4 cup grated Parmesan cheese
- 2 teaspoons dried basil
- 2 teaspoons active dry yeast

Instructions:

1. Add ingredients to the bread machine following the manufacturer's guidelines.
2. Choose the specialty bread setting and start the machine.
3. Once baked, cool the sun-dried tomato and Parmesan bread on a wire rack before slicing.

Nutritional Value (per slice):

- Calories: 130
- Protein: 4g

- Carbohydrates: 22g
- Fat: 3g
- Fiber: 2g

Cranberry Pecan Bread

Prep Time: 20 minutes
Cook Time: 3 hours
Serving Size: 12 slices

Ingredients:

- 1 1/3 cups warm water
- 2 tablespoons honey
- 1 1/2 teaspoons salt
- 3 1/2 cups bread flour
- 1/2 cup dried cranberries
- 1/2 cup chopped pecans
- 2 tablespoons orange zest
- 2 teaspoons active dry yeast

Instructions:

1. Add ingredients to the bread machine following the manufacturer's guidelines.
2. Choose the specialty bread setting and start the machine.
3. Once baked, cool the cranberry pecan bread on a wire rack before slicing.

Nutritional Value (per slice):

- Calorics: 140
- Protein: 4g

- Carbohydrates: 24g
- Fat: 3g
- Fiber: 2g

Cheddar Jalapeño Bread

Prep Time: 15 minutes
Cook Time: 3 hours
Serving Size: 14 slices

Ingredients:

- 1 1/4 cups warm milk
- 2 tablespoons unsalted butter, softened
- 1 1/2 teaspoons salt
- 3 1/4 cups bread flour
- 1 1/2 cups shredded sharp cheddar cheese
- 2 tablespoons diced pickled jalapeños
- 2 teaspoons dried parsley
- 2 teaspoons active dry yeast

Instructions:

1. Add ingredients to the bread machine following the manufacturer's guidelines.
2. Choose the specialty bread setting and start the machine.
3. Once baked, cool the cheddar jalapeño bread on a wire rack before slicing.

Nutritional Value (per slice):

- Calories: 160
- Protein: 5g

- Carbohydrates: 23g
- Fat: 5g
- Fiber: 1g

Fig and Walnut Bread

Prep Time: 20 minutes
Cook Time: 3 hours
Serving Size: 16 slices

Ingredients:

- 1 1/3 cups warm water
- 2 tablespoons honey
- 1 1/2 teaspoons salt
- 1 cup dried figs, chopped
- 1/2 cup chopped walnuts
- 3 1/2 cups bread flour
- 2 teaspoons active dry yeast

Instructions:

1. Add ingredients to the bread machine following the manufacturer's guidelines.
2. Choose the specialty bread setting and start the machine.
3. Once baked, cool the fig and walnut bread on a wire rack before slicing.

Nutritional Value (per slice):

- Calories: 120
- Protein: 4g
- Carbohydrates: 22g

- Fat: 2.5g
- Fiber: 2g

Pesto and Sun-Dried Tomato Bread

Prep Time: 15 minutes
Cook Time: 3 hours
Serving Size: 12 slices

Ingredients:

- 1 1/4 cups warm water
- 2 tablespoons olive oil
- 1 1/2 teaspoons salt
- 3 1/2 cups bread flour
- 2 tablespoons pesto sauce
- 1/4 cup chopped sun-dried tomatoes
- 2 teaspoons active dry yeast

Instructions:

1. Add ingredients to the bread machine following the manufacturer's guidelines.
2. Choose the specialty bread setting and start the machine.
3. Once baked, cool the pesto and sun-dried tomato bread on a wire rack before slicing.

Nutritional Value (per slice):

- Calories: 130
- Protein: 3g
- Carbohydrates: 23g
- Fat: 2.5g

- Fiber: 1g

Maple Bacon Bread

Prep Time: 20 minutes
Cook Time: 3 hours
Serving Size: 14 slices

Ingredients:

- 1 1/3 cups warm milk
- 2 tablespoons maple syrup
- 1 1/2 teaspoons salt
- 3 1/4 cups bread flour
- 1/2 cup cooked and crumbled bacon
- 2 tablespoons unsalted butter, melted
- 2 teaspoons active dry yeast

Instructions:

1. Add ingredients to the bread machine following the manufacturer's guidelines.
2. Choose the specialty bread setting and start the machine.
3. Once baked, cool the maple bacon bread on a wire rack before slicing.

Nutritional Value (per slice):

- Calories: 150
- Protein: 5g
- Carbohydrates: 23g
- Fat: 4g
- Fiber: 1g

Caramelized Onion and Gruyère Bread

Prep Time: 15 minutes
Cook Time: 3 hours
Serving Size: 16 slices

Ingredients:

- 1 1/4 cups warm water
- 2 tablespoons olive oil
- 1 1/2 teaspoons salt
- 3 1/2 cups bread flour
- 1 cup caramelized onions
- 1 cup shredded Gruyère cheese
- 2 teaspoons active dry yeast

Instructions:

1. Add ingredients to the bread machine following the manufacturer's guidelines.
2. Choose the specialty bread setting and start the machine.
3. Once baked, cool the caramelized onion and Gruyère bread on a wire rack before slicing.

Nutritional Value (per slice):

- Calories: 140
- Protein: 5g
- Carbohydrates: 22g
- Fat: 3g
- Fiber: 1g

Multigrain Seeded Bread

Prep Time: 20 minutes
Cook Time: 3 hours
Serving Size: 14 slices

Ingredients:

- 1 1/3 cups warm water
- 2 tablespoons honey
- 1 1/2 teaspoons salt
- 2 cups bread flour
- 1 cup whole wheat flour
- 1/4 cup flaxseeds
- 1/4 cup sunflower seeds
- 1/4 cup pumpkin seeds
- 2 teaspoons active dry yeast

Instructions:

1. Add ingredients to the bread machine following the manufacturer's guidelines.
2. Choose the multigrain setting and start the machine.
3. Once baked, cool the multigrain seeded bread on a wire rack before slicing.

Nutritional Value (per slice):

- Calories: 130
- Protein: 4g
- Carbohydrates: 22g
- Fat: 3g
- Fiber: 4g

Herb and Cheese Fougasse

Prep Time: 25 minutes
Cook Time: 3 hours
Serving Size: 12 slices

Ingredients:

- 1 1/4 cups warm water
- 2 tablespoons olive oil
- 1 1/2 teaspoons salt
- 3 1/2 cups bread flour
- 1 cup grated Parmesan cheese
- 2 tablespoons chopped fresh rosemary
- 2 teaspoons dried thyme
- 2 teaspoons active dry yeast

Instructions:

1. Add ingredients to the bread machine following the manufacturer's guidelines.
2. Choose the fougasse setting and start the machine.
3. Once baked, cool the herb and cheese fougasse on a wire rack before slicing.

Nutritional Value (per slice):

- Calories: 140
- Protein: 5g
- Carbohydrates: 22g
- Fat: 3g
- Fiber: 1.5g

Sourdough Rye Bread

Prep Time: 15 minutes (plus sourdough starter preparation)
Cook Time: 3 hours
Serving Size: 16 slices

Ingredients:

- 1 1/3 cups active sourdough starter
- 1 1/4 cups warm water
- 1 1/2 teaspoons salt
- 2 cups bread flour
- 1 cup rye flour
- 1 tablespoon caraway seeds
- 2 teaspoons active dry yeast

Instructions:

1. Prepare the sourdough starter in advance.
2. Add ingredients to the bread machine following the manufacturer's guidelines.
3. Choose the sourdough setting and start the machine.
4. Once baked, cool the sourdough rye bread on a wire rack before slicing.

Nutritional Value (per slice):

- Calories: 110
- Protein: 3g
- Carbohydrates: 21g
- Fat: 1g
- Fiber: 2.5g

Garlic and Herb Knots

Prep Time: 15 minutes
Cook Time: 2 hours 30 minutes
Serving Size: 16 knots

Ingredients:

- 1 cup warm water
- 2 tablespoons olive oil
- 1 1/2 teaspoons salt
- 3 1/2 cups bread flour
- 3 cloves garlic, minced
- 2 tablespoons chopped fresh parsley
- 2 teaspoons dried oregano
- 2 teaspoons active dry yeast

Instructions:

1. Add ingredients to the bread machine following the manufacturer's guidelines.
2. Choose the dough setting and start the machine.
3. Once the dough is ready, divide it into 16 portions, roll each portion into a rope, and tie into knots.
4. Place the knots on a baking sheet, let them rise for 30 minutes, and bake in a preheated oven at 375°F (190°C) for 15-18 minutes or until golden brown.
5. Allow the garlic and herb knots to cool slightly before serving.

Nutritional Value (per knot):

- Calories: 100
- Protein: 3g

- Carbohydrates: 18g
- Fat: 2g
- Fiber: 1g

Chocolate Cherry Brioche

Prep Time: 25 minutes
Cook Time: 3 hours
Serving Size: 12 slices

Ingredients:

- 1/2 cup warm milk
- 2 tablespoons sugar
- 1 1/2 teaspoons salt
- 3 cups bread flour
- 1/4 cup unsalted butter, softened
- 2 eggs
- 1/2 cup dried cherries
- 1/2 cup chocolate chips
- 2 teaspoons active dry yeast

Instructions:

1. Add ingredients to the bread machine following the manufacturer's guidelines.
2. Choose the brioche setting and start the machine.
3. Once baked, cool the chocolate cherry brioche on a wire rack before slicing.

Nutritional Value (per slice):

- Calories: 180

- Protein: 4g
- Carbohydrates: 25g
- Fat: 7g
- Fiber: 2g

Prosciutto and Parmesan Focaccia

Prep Time: 20 minutes
Cook Time: 3 hours
Serving Size: 14 slices

Ingredients:

- 1 1/3 cups warm water
- 2 tablespoons olive oil
- 1 1/2 teaspoons salt
- 3 1/2 cups bread flour
- 1/4 cup grated Parmesan cheese
- 3 ounces prosciutto, thinly sliced
- 2 teaspoons dried thyme
- 2 teaspoons active dry yeast

Instructions:

1. Add ingredients to the bread machine following the manufacturer's guidelines.
2. Choose the focaccia setting and start the machine.
3. Once baked, cool the prosciutto and Parmesan focaccia on a wire rack before slicing.

Nutritional Value (per slice):

- Calories: 140

- Protein: 5g
- Carbohydrates: 20g
- Fat: 4g
- Fiber: 1g

Chapter Four

Gluten-Free Breads

Classic Gluten-Free White Bread

Prep Time: 15 minutes
Cook Time: 2 hours 30 minutes
Serving Size: 12 slices

Ingredients:

- 2 1/4 cups gluten-free all-purpose flour
- 1 teaspoon xanthan gum
- 1 1/2 teaspoons salt
- 2 tablespoons sugar
- 1 1/2 teaspoons active dry yeast
- 1 1/4 cups warm water
- 2 tablespoons olive oil
- 3 eggs

Instructions:

1. Add ingredients to the bread machine following the manufacturer's guidelines.
2. Choose the gluten-free setting and start the machine.
3. Once baked, cool the gluten-free white bread on a wire rack before slicing.

Nutritional Value (per slice):

- Calories: 120
- Protein: 2g
- Carbohydrates: 20g

- Fat: 4g
- Fiber: 1g

Chia Seed and Quinoa Bread

Prep Time: 20 minutes
Cook Time: 3 hours
Serving Size: 14 slices

Ingredients:

- 2 cups gluten-free all-purpose flour
- 1/2 cup quinoa flour
- 1/4 cup chia seeds
- 1 1/2 teaspoons baking powder
- 1 1/2 teaspoons salt
- 2 tablespoons honey
- 1 1/4 cups warm almond milk
- 2 tablespoons olive oil
- 2 teaspoons active dry yeast

Instructions:

1. Add ingredients to the bread machine following the manufacturer's guidelines.
2. Choose the gluten-free setting and start the machine.
3. Once baked, cool the chia seed and quinoa bread on a wire rack before slicing.

Nutritional Value (per slice):

- Calories: 140
- Protein: 3g

- Carbohydrates: 22g
- Fat: 5g
- Fiber: 2g

Almond Flour Banana Bread

Prep Time: 15 minutes
Cook Time: 3 hours
Serving Size: 12 slices

Ingredients:

- 2 cups almond flour
- 1/4 cup coconut flour
- 1 1/2 teaspoons baking soda
- 1/2 teaspoon salt
- 3 ripe bananas, mashed
- 3 eggs
- 1/4 cup coconut oil, melted
- 2 teaspoons vanilla extract
- 2 teaspoons apple cider vinegar
- 2 teaspoons active dry yeast

Instructions:

1. Add ingredients to the bread machine following the manufacturer's guidelines.
2. Choose the gluten-free setting and start the machine.
3. Once baked, cool the almond flour banana bread on a wire rack before slicing.

Nutritional Value (per slice):

- Calories: 180
- Protein: 5g
- Carbohydrates: 15g
- Fat: 12g
- Fiber: 3g

Sweet Potato and Walnut Bread

Prep Time: 20 minutes
Cook Time: 3 hours
Serving Size: 16 slices

Ingredients:

- 2 cups mashed sweet potatoes
- 2 cups gluten-free all-purpose flour
- 1/4 cup almond flour
- 1/2 cup chopped walnuts
- 1/4 cup maple syrup
- 1 1/2 teaspoons baking powder
- 1/2 teaspoon baking soda
- 1/2 teaspoon salt
- 2 teaspoons cinnamon
- 3 eggs
- 1/4 cup melted coconut oil
- 2 teaspoons active dry yeast

Instructions:

1. Add ingredients to the bread machine following the manufacturer's guidelines.
2. Choose the gluten-free setting and start the machine.
3. Once baked, cool the sweet potato and walnut bread on a wire rack before slicing.

Nutritional Value (per slice):

- Calories: 150
- Protein: 4g
- Carbohydrates: 22g
- Fat: 6g
- Fiber: 3g

Spinach and Feta Socca Bread

Prep Time: 15 minutes
Cook Time: 2 hours
Serving Size: 12 slices

Ingredients:

- 2 cups chickpea flour
- 1 1/2 teaspoons baking powder
- 1/2 teaspoon salt
- 1 1/4 cups water
- 2 tablespoons olive oil
- 1 cup fresh spinach, chopped
- 1/2 cup crumbled feta cheese
- 2 teaspoons dried oregano
- 2 teaspoons active dry yeast

Instructions:

1. Add ingredients to the bread machine following the manufacturer's guidelines.
2. Choose the gluten-free setting and start the machine.
3. Once baked, cool the spinach and feta socca bread on a wire rack before slicing.

Nutritional Value (per slice):

- Calories: 110
- Protein: 5g
- Carbohydrates: 13g
- Fat: 5g
- Fiber: 2g

Hazelnut and Fig Bread

Prep Time: 20 minutes
Cook Time: 3 hours
Serving Size: 14 slices

Ingredients:

- 2 cups gluten-free all-purpose flour
- 1/2 cup hazelnut flour
- 1/2 cup dried figs, chopped
- 1/4 cup honey
- 1 1/2 teaspoons baking powder
- 1/2 teaspoon salt
- 1 1/4 cups almond milk
- 2 tablespoons olive oil

- 2 eggs
- 2 teaspoons active dry yeast

Instructions:

1. Add ingredients to the bread machine following the manufacturer's guidelines.
2. Choose the gluten-free setting and start the machine.
3. Once baked, cool the hazelnut and fig bread on a wire rack before slicing.

Nutritional Value (per slice):

- Calories: 160
- Protein: 4g
- Carbohydrates: 22g
- Fat: 6g

Cranberry Orange Quinoa Bread

Prep Time: 20 minutes
Cook Time: 3 hours
Serving Size: 12 slices

Ingredients:

- 2 cups gluten-free all-purpose flour
- 1/2 cup quinoa flour
- 1/2 cup dried cranberries
- Zest of one orange
- 1 1/2 teaspoons baking powder
- 1/2 teaspoon salt
- 1 1/4 cups orange juice

- 2 tablespoons olive oil
- 2 tablespoons honey
- 2 teaspoons active dry yeast

Instructions:

1. Add ingredients to the bread machine following the manufacturer's guidelines.
2. Choose the gluten-free setting and start the machine.
3. Once baked, cool the cranberry orange quinoa bread on a wire rack before slicing.

Nutritional Value (per slice):

- Calories: 140
- Protein: 3g
- Carbohydrates: 24g
- Fat: 3.5g
- Fiber: 2g

Rosemary Parmesan Chickpea Bread

Prep Time: 15 minutes
Cook Time: 2 hours 30 minutes
Serving Size: 14 slices

Ingredients:

- 2 cups chickpea flour
- 1 1/2 teaspoons baking powder
- 1/2 teaspoon salt
- 1 1/4 cups water
- 2 tablespoons olive oil

- 2 tablespoons fresh rosemary, chopped
- 1/4 cup grated Parmesan cheese
- 2 teaspoons active dry yeast

Instructions:

1. Add ingredients to the bread machine following the manufacturer's guidelines.
2. Choose the gluten-free setting and start the machine.
3. Once baked, cool the rosemary Parmesan chickpea bread on a wire rack before slicing.

Nutritional Value (per slice):

- Calories: 110
- Protein: 4g
- Carbohydrates: 15g
- Fat: 4g
- Fiber: 2g

Pumpkin Seed and Teff Bread

Prep Time: 20 minutes
Cook Time: 3 hours
Serving Size: 16 slices

Ingredients:

- 1 1/2 cups teff flour
- 1/2 cup gluten-free all-purpose flour
- 1/2 cup pumpkin seeds
- 1 1/2 teaspoons baking powder

- 1/2 teaspoon salt
- 1 1/4 cups water
- 2 tablespoons olive oil
- 2 tablespoons maple syrup
- 2 teaspoons active dry yeast

Instructions:

1. Add ingredients to the bread machine following the manufacturer's guidelines.
2. Choose the gluten-free setting and start the machine.
3. Once baked, cool the pumpkin seed and teff bread on a wire rack before slicing.

Nutritional Value (per slice):

- Calories: 120
- Protein: 4g
- Carbohydrates: 20g
- Fat: 3g
- Fiber: 2g

Coconut Flour Banana Bread

Prep Time: 15 minutes
Cook Time: 3 hours
Serving Size: 12 slices

Ingredients:

- 1 1/2 cups coconut flour
- 1/2 cup almond flour

- 1 1/2 teaspoons baking powder
- 1/2 teaspoon salt
- 3 ripe bananas, mashed
- 4 eggs
- 1/4 cup coconut oil, melted
- 1/4 cup maple syrup
- 2 teaspoons vanilla extract
- 2 teaspoons active dry yeast

Instructions:

1. Add ingredients to the bread machine following the manufacturer's guidelines.
2. Choose the gluten-free setting and start the machine.
3. Once baked, cool the coconut flour banana bread on a wire rack before slicing.

Nutritional Value (per slice):

- Calories: 160
- Protein: 4g
- Carbohydrates: 19g
- Fat: 8g
- Fiber: 4g

Sorghum and Seed Bread

Prep Time: 20 minutes
Cook Time: 3 hours
Serving Size: 14 slices

Ingredients:

- 1 1/2 cups sorghum flour
- 1/2 cup gluten-free all-purpose flour
- 1/4 cup sunflower seeds
- 1/4 cup pumpkin seeds
- 1 1/2 teaspoons baking powder
- 1/2 teaspoon salt
- 1 1/4 cups water
- 2 tablespoons olive oil
- 2 tablespoons honey
- 2 teaspoons active dry yeast

Instructions:

1. Add ingredients to the bread machine following the manufacturer's guidelines.
2. Choose the gluten-free setting and start the machine.
3. Once baked, cool the sorghum and seed bread on a wire rack before slicing.

Nutritional Value (per slice):

- Calories: 130
- Protein: 3g
- Carbohydrates: 20g
- Fat: 5g

- Fiber: 2g

Raspberry Almond Flour Bread

Prep Time: 15 minutes
Cook Time: 3 hours
Serving Size: 16 slices

Ingredients:

- 1 1/2 cups almond flour
- 1/2 cup gluten-free all-purpose flour
- 1/2 cup fresh or frozen raspberries
- 1 1/2 teaspoons baking powder
- 1/2 teaspoon salt
- 1/4 cup coconut oil, melted
- 1/4 cup honey
- 1 teaspoon almond extract
- 3 eggs
- 2 teaspoons active dry yeast

Instructions:

1. Add ingredients to the bread machine following the manufacturer's guidelines.
2. Choose the gluten-free setting and start the machine.
3. Once baked, cool the raspberry almond flour bread on a wire rack before slicing.

Nutritional Value (per slice):

- Calories: 140
- Protein: 4g
- Carbohydrates: 16g

- Fat: 7g
- Fiber: 2g

Millet and Sun-Dried Tomato Bread

Prep Time: 20 minutes
Cook Time: 3 hours
Serving Size: 12 slices

Ingredients:

- 1 1/2 cups millet flour
- 1/2 cup gluten-free all-purpose flour
- 1/4 cup sun-dried tomatoes, chopped
- 1 1/2 teaspoons baking powder
- 1/2 teaspoon salt
- 1 1/4 cups water
- 2 tablespoons olive oil
- 2 teaspoons apple cider vinegar
- 2 teaspoons active dry yeast

Instructions:

1. Add ingredients to the bread machine following the manufacturer's guidelines.
2. Choose the gluten-free setting and start the machine.
3. Once baked, cool the millet and sun-dried tomato bread on a wire rack before slicing.

Nutritional Value (per slice):

- Calories: 130
- Protein: 3g
- Carbohydrates: 22g

- Fat: 4g
- Fiber: 2g

Pistachio and Cranberry Bread

Prep Time: 15 minutes
Cook Time: 3 hours
Serving Size: 14 slices

Ingredients:

- 1 1/2 cups gluten-free all-purpose flour
- 1/2 cup pistachio flour
- 1/4 cup dried cranberries
- 1 1/2 teaspoons baking powder
- 1/2 teaspoon salt
- 1 1/4 cups almond milk
- 2 tablespoons olive oil
- 2 tablespoons maple syrup
- 2 teaspoons active dry yeast

Instructions:

1. Add ingredients to the bread machine following the manufacturer's guidelines.
2. Choose the gluten-free setting and start the machine.
3. Once baked, cool the pistachio and cranberry bread on a wire rack before slicing.

Nutritional Value (per slice):

- Calories: 140
- Protein: 3g
- Carbohydrates: 23g

- Fat: 5g
- Fiber: 2g

Buckwheat and Date Bread

Prep Time: 20 minutes
Cook Time: 3 hours
Serving Size: 16 slices

Ingredients:

- 1 1/2 cups buckwheat flour
- 1/2 cup gluten-free all-purpose flour
- 1/2 cup chopped dates
- 1 1/2 teaspoons baking powder
- 1/2 teaspoon salt
- 1 1/4 cups water
- 2 tablespoons olive oil
- 2 tablespoons honey
- 2 teaspoons active dry yeast

Instructions:

1. Add ingredients to the bread machine following the manufacturer's guidelines.
2. Choose the gluten-free setting and start the machine.
3. Once baked, cool the buckwheat and date bread on a wire rack before slicing.

Nutritional Value (per slice):

- Calories: 120
- Protein: 3g
- Carbohydrates: 23g
- Fat: 2.5g
- Fiber: 2.5g

Chapter Five

Artisan Breads

Classic French Baguette

Prep Time: 15 minutes
Cook Time: 2 hours 30 minutes
Serving Size: 2 baguettes

Ingredients:

- 3 1/2 cups bread flour
- 1 1/2 teaspoons salt
- 1 1/4 cups warm water
- 1 tablespoon sugar
- 2 teaspoons active dry yeast

Instructions:

1. Add ingredients to the bread machine following the manufacturer's guidelines.
2. Choose the French bread setting and start the machine.
3. Once the dough is ready, shape it into two baguettes, let them rise for 30 minutes, and bake in a preheated oven at 400°F (200°C) for 20-25 minutes or until golden brown.
4. Cool the French baguettes on a wire rack before serving.

Nutritional Value (per serving):

- Calories: 150
- Protein: 4g
- Carbohydrates: 30g
- Fat: 1g

- Fiber: 1g

Italian Ciabatta

Prep Time: 20 minutes
Cook Time: 3 hours
Serving Size: 1 loaf

Ingredients:

- 3 cups bread flour
- 1 1/2 teaspoons salt
- 1 1/4 cups warm water
- 2 tablespoons olive oil
- 2 teaspoons sugar
- 2 teaspoons active dry yeast

Instructions:

1. Add ingredients to the bread machine following the manufacturer's guidelines.
2. Choose the Italian bread setting and start the machine.
3. Once the dough is ready, transfer it to a well-floured surface, shape it into a rectangle, and let it rise for 30 minutes.
4. Bake the ciabatta in a preheated oven at 425°F (220°C) for 25-30 minutes or until golden brown.
5. Cool the Italian ciabatta on a wire rack before slicing.

Nutritional Value (per serving):

- Calories: 160
- Protein: 4g

- Carbohydrates: 30g
- Fat: 3g
- Fiber: 1g

Sourdough Artisan Boule

Prep Time: 15 minutes (plus sourdough starter preparation)
Cook Time: 3 hours
Serving Size: 1 boule

Ingredients:

- 2 1/2 cups bread flour
- 1/2 cup whole wheat flour
- 1 1/2 teaspoons salt
- 1 1/4 cups active sourdough starter
- 1/2 cup warm water
- 2 teaspoons honey

Instructions:

1. Prepare the sourdough starter in advance.
2. Add ingredients to the bread machine following the manufacturer's guidelines.
3. Choose the sourdough setting and start the machine.
4. Once the dough is ready, transfer it to a floured surface, shape it into a boule, and let it rise for 1-2 hours.
5. Bake the sourdough boule in a preheated oven at 400°F (200°C) for 30-35 minutes or until the crust is golden.
6. Cool the sourdough boule on a wire rack before slicing.

Nutritional Value (per serving):

- Calories: 180
- Protein: 5g
- Carbohydrates: 35g
- Fat: 1g
- Fiber: 2g

Whole Grain Seeded Bread

Prep Time: 20 minutes
Cook Time: 3 hours
Serving Size: 1 loaf

Ingredients:

- 2 cups whole wheat flour
- 1 cup bread flour
- 1/4 cup sunflower seeds
- 1/4 cup pumpkin seeds
- 2 tablespoons flaxseeds
- 1 1/2 teaspoons salt
- 1 1/4 cups warm water
- 2 tablespoons olive oil
- 2 teaspoons honey
- 2 teaspoons active dry yeast

Instructions:

1. Add ingredients to the bread machine following the manufacturer's guidelines.

2. Choose the whole grain setting and start the machine.

3. Once the dough is ready, transfer it to a lightly floured surface, shape it into a loaf, and let it rise for 30 minutes.

4. Bake the whole grain seeded bread in a preheated oven at 375°F (190°C) for 35-40 minutes or until the crust is golden.

5. Cool the bread on a wire rack before slicing.

Nutritional Value (per serving):

- Calories: 160
- Protein: 5g
- Carbohydrates: 30g
- Fat: 4g
- Fiber: 5g

Rosemary and Olive No-Knead Bread

Prep Time: 10 minutes (plus resting time)
Cook Time: 3 hours
Serving Size: 1 round loaf

Ingredients:

- 3 cups bread flour
- 1 1/2 teaspoons salt
- 1 1/4 cups warm water
- 1 tablespoon olive oil
- 2 teaspoons dried rosemary
- 1/2 cup pitted and sliced Kalamata olives

- 2 teaspoons active dry yeast

Instructions:

1. Add ingredients to the bread machine following the manufacturer's guidelines.
2. Choose the artisan or no-knead setting and start the machine.
3. Once the dough is ready, transfer it to a floured surface, shape it into a round loaf, and let it rest for 30 minutes.
4. Bake the rosemary and olive bread in a preheated oven at 400°F (200°C) for 30-35 minutes or until the crust is crusty.
5. Cool the bread on a wire rack before slicing.

Nutritional Value (per serving):

- Calories: 180
- Protein: 4g
- Carbohydrates: 35g
- Fat: 3g
- Fiber: 2g

Cranberry Walnut Artisan Bread

Prep Time: 15 minutes
Cook Time: 3 hours
Serving Size: 1 boule

Ingredients:

- 2 1/2 cups bread flour
- 1/2 cup whole wheat flour
- 1 1/2 teaspoons salt

- 1 1/4 cups warm water
- 2 tablespoons honey
- 1/2 cup dried cranberries
- 1/2 cup chopped walnuts
- 2 teaspoons active dry yeast

Instructions:

1. Add ingredients to the bread machine following the manufacturer's guidelines.
2. Choose the artisan bread setting and start the machine.
3. Once the dough is ready, transfer it to a floured surface, shape it into a boule, and let it rise for 1-2 hours.
4. Bake the cranberry walnut artisan bread in a preheated oven at 375°F (190°C) for 35-40 minutes or until the crust is golden.
5. Cool the bread on a wire rack before slicing.

Nutritional Value (per serving):

- Calories: 190
- Protein: 5g
- Carbohydrates: 35g
- Fat: 4g
- Fiber: 3g

Rustic Rye Bread

Prep Time: 15 minutes
Cook Time: 3 hours
Serving Size: 1 loaf

Ingredients:

- 2 cups rye flour
- 1 cup bread flour
- 1 1/2 teaspoons salt
- 1 1/4 cups warm water
- 2 tablespoons molasses
- 1 tablespoon caraway seeds
- 2 teaspoons active dry yeast

Instructions:

1. Add ingredients to the bread machine following the manufacturer's guidelines.
2. Choose the rye bread setting and start the machine.
3. Once the dough is ready, transfer it to a lightly floured surface, shape it into a loaf, and let it rise for 30 minutes.
4. Bake the rustic rye bread in a preheated oven at 375°F (190°C) for 40-45 minutes or until the crust is firm.
5. Cool the bread on a wire rack before slicing.

Nutritional Value (per serving):

- Calories: 160
- Protein: 4g
- Carbohydrates: 30g

- Fat: 2g
- Fiber: 4g

Sun-Dried Tomato and Basil Fougasse

Prep Time: 20 minutes
Cook Time: 2 hours 30 minutes
Serving Size: 1 fougasse

Ingredients:

- 3 cups bread flour
- 1 1/2 teaspoons salt
- 1 1/4 cups warm water
- 2 tablespoons olive oil
- 2 teaspoons sugar
- 1/4 cup sun-dried tomatoes, chopped
- 2 tablespoons fresh basil, chopped
- 2 teaspoons active dry yeast

Instructions:

1. Add ingredients to the bread machine following the manufacturer's guidelines.
2. Choose the artisan or fougasse setting and start the machine.
3. Once the dough is ready, transfer it to a parchment-lined baking sheet, shape it into a fougasse, and let it rise for 30 minutes.
4. Bake the sun-dried tomato and basil fougasse in a preheated oven at 400°F (200°C) for 25-30 minutes or until golden.
5. Cool the fougasse on a wire rack before serving.

Nutritional Value (per serving):

- Calories: 170
- Protein: 5g
- Carbohydrates: 30g
- Fat: 4g
- Fiber: 2g

Herb and Cheese Swirl Bread

Prep Time: 15 minutes
Cook Time: 3 hours
Serving Size: 1 loaf

Ingredients:

- 3 cups bread flour
- 1 1/2 teaspoons salt
- 1 1/4 cups warm milk
- 2 tablespoons unsalted butter, melted
- 2 teaspoons sugar
- 1 tablespoon mixed dried herbs (rosemary, thyme, oregano)
- 1/2 cup shredded sharp cheddar cheese
- 2 teaspoons active dry yeast

Instructions:

1. Add ingredients to the bread machine following the manufacturer's guidelines.
2. Choose the artisan or swirl bread setting and start the machine.
3. Once the dough is ready, transfer it to a greased loaf pan, sprinkle with extra cheese, and let it rise for 30 minutes.

4. Bake the herb and cheese swirl bread in a preheated oven at 375°F (190°C) for 35-40 minutes or until the top is golden.

5. Cool the bread in the pan for 10 minutes, then transfer it to a wire rack to cool completely.

Nutritional Value (per serving):

- Calories: 190
- Protein: 6g
- Carbohydrates: 30g
- Fat: 5g
- Fiber: 2g

Multigrain Harvest Loaf

Prep Time: 20 minutes
Cook Time: 3 hours
Serving Size: 1 loaf

Ingredients:

- 1 1/2 cups bread flour
- 1 cup whole wheat flour
- 1/2 cup oats
- 1/4 cup flaxseeds
- 1 1/2 teaspoons salt
- 1 1/4 cups warm water
- 2 tablespoons honey
- 2 tablespoons olive oil

- 2 teaspoons active dry yeast

Instructions:

1. Add ingredients to the bread machine following the manufacturer's guidelines.
2. Choose the multigrain or whole grain setting and start the machine.
3. Once the dough is ready, transfer it to a greased loaf pan, let it rise for 30 minutes, and bake in a preheated oven at 375°F (190°C) for 35-40 minutes or until golden.
4. Cool the multigrain harvest loaf on a wire rack before slicing.

Nutritional Value (per serving):

- Calories: 180
- Protein: 5g
- Carbohydrates: 30g
- Fat: 5g
- Fiber: 4g

Walnut and Fig Artisan Bread

Prep Time: 15 minutes
Cook Time: 3 hours
Serving Size: 1 boule

Ingredients:

- 2 1/2 cups bread flour
- 1/2 cup whole wheat flour
- 1 1/2 teaspoons salt
- 1 1/4 cups warm water
- 2 tablespoons honey

- 1/2 cup chopped walnuts
- 1/2 cup chopped dried figs
- 2 teaspoons active dry yeast

Instructions:

1. Add ingredients to the bread machine following the manufacturer's guidelines.
2. Choose the artisan or boule setting and start the machine.
3. Once the dough is ready, transfer it to a floured surface, shape it into a boule, and let it rise for 1-2 hours.
4. Bake the walnut and fig artisan bread in a preheated oven at 375°F (190°C) for 35-40 minutes or until the crust is golden.
5. Cool the bread on a wire rack before slicing.

Nutritional Value (per serving):

- Calories: 200
- Protein: 6g
- Carbohydrates: 35g
- Fat: 5g
- Fiber: 3g

Caramelized Onion and Gruyere Fougasse

Prep Time: 20 minutes
Cook Time: 2 hours 30 minutes
Serving Size: 1 fougasse

Ingredients:

- 3 cups bread flour

- 1 1/2 teaspoons salt
- 1 1/4 cups warm water
- 2 tabspoons olive oil
- 1 teaspoon sugar
- 1 cup caramelized onions
- 1/2 cup shredded Gruyere cheese
- 2 teaspoons active dry yeast

Instructions:

1. Add ingredients to the bread machine following the manufacturer's guidelines.
2. Choose the artisan or fougasse setting and start the machine.
3. Once the dough is ready, transfer it to a parchment-lined baking sheet, shape it into a fougasse, and top with caramelized onions and Gruyere cheese.
4. Let it rise for 30 minutes, then bake in a preheated oven at 400°F (200°C) for 25-30 minutes or until golden.
5. Cool the caramelized onion and Gruyere fougasse on a wire rack before serving.

Nutritional Value (per serving):

- Calories: 220
- Protein: 8g
- Carbohydrates: 35g
- Fat: 6g
- Fiber: 2g

Cranberry Pecan Sourdough Bread

Prep Time: 20 minutes (plus sourdough starter preparation)
Cook Time: 3 hours
Serving Size: 1 boule

Ingredients:

- 2 1/2 cups bread flour
- 1/2 cup whole wheat flour
- 1 1/2 teaspoons salt
- 1 1/4 cups active sourdough starter
- 1/2 cup warm water
- 2 tablespoons honey
- 1/2 cup dried cranberries
- 1/2 cup chopped pecans
- 2 teaspoons active dry yeast

Instructions:

1. Prepare the sourdough starter in advance.
2. Add ingredients to the bread machine following the manufacturer's guidelines.
3. Choose the artisan or boule setting and start the machine.
4. Once the dough is ready, transfer it to a floured surface, shape it into a boule, and let it rise for 1-2 hours.
5. Bake the cranberry pecan sourdough bread in a preheated oven at 375°F (190°C) for 35-40 minutes or until the crust is golden.
6. Cool the bread on a wire rack before slicing.

Nutritional Value (per serving):

- Calories: 210
- Protein: 6g
- Carbohydrates: 40g
- Fat: 4g
- Fiber: 3g

Garlic and Herb Focaccia

Prep Time: 20 minutes
Cook Time: 2 hours 30 minutes
Serving Size: 1 focaccia

Ingredients:

- 3 cups bread flour
- 1 1/2 teaspoons salt
- 1 1/4 cups warm water
- 2 tablespoons olive oil
- 2 teaspoons sugar
- 2 cloves garlic, minced
- 1 tablespoon mixed dried herbs (rosemary, thyme, oregano)
- Sea salt for topping
- 2 teaspoons active dry yeast

Instructions:

1. Add ingredients to the bread machine following the manufacturer's guidelines.
2. Choose the artisan or focaccia setting and start the machine.

3. Once the dough is ready, transfer it to a greased baking sheet, shape it into a rectangle, and let it rise for 30 minutes.

4. Create dimples on the dough's surface, brush with olive oil, sprinkle minced garlic, herbs, and sea salt.

5. Bake the garlic and herb focaccia in a preheated oven at 400°F (200°C) for 20-25 minutes or until golden brown.

6. Cool the focaccia on a wire rack before slicing.

Nutritional Value (per serving):

- Calories: 180
- Protein: 5g
- Carbohydrates: 30g
- Fat: 5g
- Fiber: 2g

Challah Bread with Sesame Seeds

Prep Time: 25 minutes
Cook Time: 3 hours
Serving Size: 1 loaf

Ingredients:

- 3 cups bread flour
- 1/4 cup sugar
- 1 1/2 teaspoons salt
- 1/4 cup unsalted butter, melted
- 3 large eggs
- 1/2 cup warm water

- 2 teaspoons active dry yeast
- Sesame seeds for topping

Instructions:

1. Add ingredients to the bread machine following the manufacturer's guidelines.
2. Choose the artisan or sweet bread setting and start the machine.
3. Once the dough is ready, transfer it to a floured surface, braid it into a challah shape, and let it rise for 30 minutes.
4. Brush the top with egg wash and sprinkle sesame seeds.
5. Bake the challah bread in a preheated oven at 350°F (180°C) for 30-35 minutes or until golden brown.
6. Cool the bread on a wire rack before slicing.

Nutritional Value (per serving):

- Calories: 190
- Protein: 5g
- Carbohydrates: 30g
- Fat: 6g
- Fiber: 1g

Chapter Six

Holiday and Special Occasion Breads

Cranberry Orange Walnut Bread

Prep Time: 20 minutes
Cook Time: 3 hours
Serving Size: 1 loaf

Ingredients:

- 2 1/2 cups bread flour
- 1/2 cup whole wheat flour
- 1 1/2 teaspoons salt
- 1 1/4 cups warm water
- 1/4 cup orange juice
- 2 tablespoons olive oil
- 1/4 cup honey
- 1/2 cup dried cranberries
- 1/2 cup chopped walnuts
- 2 teaspoons active dry yeast
- Zest of one orange

Instructions:

1. Add ingredients to the bread machine following the manufacturer's guidelines.
2. Choose the sweet bread setting and start the machine.
3. Once the dough is ready, fold in dried cranberries, chopped walnuts, and orange zest.
4. Transfer the dough to a greased loaf pan and let it rise for 30 minutes.

5. Bake the cranberry orange walnut bread in a preheated oven at 375°F (190°C) for 35-40 minutes or until golden.
6. Cool the bread on a wire rack before slicing.

Nutritional Value (per serving):

- Calories: 190
- Protein: 4g
- Carbohydrates: 35g
- Fat: 4.5g
- Fiber: 2g

Chocolate Pecan Swirl Bread

Prep Time: 25 minutes
Cook Time: 3 hours
Serving Size: 1 loaf

Ingredients:

- 3 cups bread flour
- 1/4 cup sugar
- 1 1/2 teaspoons salt
- 1 cup warm milk
- 3 tablespoons unsalted butter, melted
- 2 teaspoons vanilla extract
- 2 teaspoons active dry yeast
- 1/2 cup chopped pecans
- 1/2 cup chocolate chips

Instructions:

1. Add ingredients to the bread machine following the manufacturer's guidelines.
2. Choose the sweet bread or swirl setting and start the machine.
3. Once the dough is ready, roll it out on a floured surface.
4. Sprinkle chopped pecans and chocolate chips over the dough, then roll it into a log.
5. Place the dough in a greased loaf pan and let it rise for 30 minutes.
6. Bake the chocolate pecan swirl bread in a preheated oven at 350°F (180°C) for 30-35 minutes or until a toothpick comes out clean.
7. Cool the bread on a wire rack before slicing.

Nutritional Value (per serving):

- Calories: 200
- Protein: 4g
- Carbohydrates: 35g
- Fat: 5g
- Fiber: 2g

Maple Pecan Pumpkin Bread

Prep Time: 20 minutes
Cook Time: 3 hours
Serving Size: 1 loaf

Ingredients:

- 2 1/2 cups bread flour
- 1/2 cup whole wheat flour
- 1 1/2 teaspoons salt

- 1 1/4 cups warm water
- 1/2 cup pumpkin puree
- 1/4 cup maple syrup
- 2 tablespoons olive oil
- 2 teaspoons pumpkin spice
- 1/2 cup chopped pecans
- 2 teaspoons active dry yeast

Instructions:

1. Add ingredients to the bread machine following the manufacturer's guidelines.
2. Choose the sweet bread setting and start the machine.
3. Once the dough is ready, fold in chopped pecans.
4. Transfer the dough to a greased loaf pan and let it rise for 30 minutes.
5. Bake the maple pecan pumpkin bread in a preheated oven at 375°F (190°C) for 35-40 minutes or until a toothpick comes out clean.
6. Cool the bread on a wire rack before slicing.

Nutritional Value (per serving):

- Calories: 180
- Protein: 4g
- Carbohydrates: 30g
- Fat: 4g
- Fiber: 2g

Rosemary and Cranberry Focaccia

Prep Time: 25 minutes
Cook Time: 2 hours 30 minutes
Serving Size: 1 focaccia

Ingredients:

- 3 cups bread flour
- 1 1/2 teaspoons salt
- 1 1/4 cups warm water
- 2 tablespoons olive oil
- 2 teaspoons sugar
- 1 tablespoon fresh rosemary, chopped
- 1/2 cup dried cranberries
- Sea salt for topping
- 2 teaspoons active dry yeast

Instructions:

1. Add ingredients to the bread machine following the manufacturer's guidelines.
2. Choose the focaccia setting and start the machine.
3. Once the dough is ready, transfer it to a greased baking sheet, shape it into a rectangle, and let it rise for 30 minutes.
4. Press your fingers into the dough to create dimples, sprinkle with rosemary, cranberries, and sea salt.
5. Bake the rosemary and cranberry focaccia in a preheated oven at 400°F (200°C) for 20-25 minutes or until golden brown.
6. Cool the focaccia on a wire rack before serving.

Nutritional Value (per serving):

- Calories: 190
- Protein: 4g
- Carbohydrates: 30g
- Fat: 5g
- Fiber: 2g

Chocolate Cherry Bread

Prep Time: 20 minutes
Cook Time: 3 hours
Serving Size: 1 loaf

Ingredients:

- 2 1/2 cups bread flour
- 1/2 cup cocoa powder
- 1 1/2 teaspoons salt
- 1 1/4 cups warm water
- 1/4 cup honey
- 2 tablespoons olive oil
- 1/2 cup dried cherries, chopped
- 1/2 cup chocolate chips
- 2 teaspoons active dry yeast

Instructions:

1. Add ingredients to the bread machine following the manufacturer's guidelines.
2. Choose the sweet bread or chocolate setting and start the machine.
3. Once the dough is ready, fold in dried cherries and chocolate chips.

4. Transfer the dough to a greased loaf pan and let it rise for 30 minutes.

5. Bake the chocolate cherry bread in a preheated oven at 350°F (180°C) for 35-40 minutes or until a toothpick comes out clean.

6. Cool the bread on a wire rack before slicing.

Nutritional Value (per serving):

- Calories: 200
- Protein: 5g
- Carbohydrates: 35g
- Fat: 5g
- Fiber: 3g

Almond and Orange Twist Bread

Prep Time: 25 minutes
Cook Time: 3 hours
Serving Size: 1 twist loaf

Ingredients:

- 3 cups bread flour
- 1/4 cup sugar
- 1 1/2 teaspoons salt
- 1 1/4 cups warm milk
- 3 tablespoons unsalted butter, melted
- 2 teaspoons almond extract
- Zest of one orange
- 1/2 cup sliced almonds

- 2 teaspoons active dry yeast

Instructions:

1. Add ingredients to the bread machine following the manufacturer's guidelines.
2. Choose the sweet bread or twist setting and start the machine.
3. Once the dough is ready, transfer it to a floured surface and roll it into a rectangle.
4. Brush the surface with melted butter, sprinkle with almond slices and orange zest.
5. Roll the dough into a log, then twist it into a loaf shape and transfer it to a greased pan.
6. Let it rise for 30 minutes, then bake the almond and orange twist bread in a preheated oven at 375°F (190°C) for 35-40 minutes or until golden.
7. Cool the bread on a wire rack before slicing.

Nutritional Value (per serving):

- Calories: 220
- Protein: 6g
- Carbohydrates: 35g
- Fat: 6g
- Fiber: 2g

Pumpkin Spice Cinnamon Swirl Bread

Prep Time: 20 minutes
Cook Time: 3 hours
Serving Size: 1 loaf

Ingredients:

- 2 1/2 cups bread flour

- 1/2 cup whole wheat flour
- 1 1/2 teaspoons salt
- 1 1/4 cups warm water
- 1/2 cup pumpkin puree
- 1/4 cup maple syrup
- 2 tablespoons olive oil
- 1 tablespoon pumpkin spice
- 1/4 cup brown sugar
- 2 teaspoons ground cinnamon
- 2 teaspoons active dry yeast

Instructions:

1. Add ingredients to the bread machine following the manufacturer's guidelines.
2. Choose the sweet bread setting and start the machine.
3. Once the dough is ready, roll it out on a floured surface.
4. Mix brown sugar, cinnamon, and sprinkle the mixture over the dough.
5. Roll the dough into a log, place it in a greased loaf pan, and let it rise for 30 minutes.
6. Bake the pumpkin spice cinnamon swirl bread in a preheated oven at 375°F (190°C) for 35-40 minutes or until a toothpick comes out clean.
7. Cool the bread on a wire rack before slicing.

Nutritional Value (per serving):

- Calories: 190
- Protein: 4g
- Carbohydrates: 35g

- Fat: 4g
- Fiber: 2g

Holiday Nutmeg Eggnog Bread

Prep Time: 25 minutes
Cook Time: 3 hours
Serving Size: 1 loaf

Ingredients:

- 3 cups bread flour
- 1/4 cup sugar
- 1 1/2 teaspoons salt
- 1 cup warm eggnog
- 3 tablespoons unsalted butter, melted
- 2 tablespoons rum extract
- 1 teaspoon ground nutmeg
- 1/2 cup raisins
- 2 teaspoons active dry yeast

Instructions:

1. Add ingredients to the bread machine following the manufacturer's guidelines.
2. Choose the sweet bread setting and start the machine.
3. Once the dough is ready, fold in raisins.
4. Transfer the dough to a greased loaf pan and let it rise for 30 minutes.
5. Bake the holiday nutmeg eggnog bread in a preheated oven at 350°F (180°C) for 35-40 minutes or until a toothpick comes out clean.

6. Cool the bread on a wire rack before slicing.

Nutritional Value (per serving):

- Calories: 200
- Protein: 5g
- Carbohydrates: 35g
- Fat: 5g
- Fiber: 2g

Caramel Pecan Monkey Bread

Prep Time: 30 minutes
Cook Time: 2 hours
Serving Size: 1 bundt-shaped loaf

Ingredients:

- 3 cups bread flour
- 1/4 cup sugar
- 1 1/2 teaspoons salt
- 1 cup warm milk
- 1/4 cup unsalted butter, melted
- 2 teaspoons vanilla extract
- 1 cup chopped pecans
- 1/2 cup brown sugar
- 1 teaspoon ground cinnamon
- 1/2 cup caramel sauce
- 2 teaspoons active dry yeast

Instructions:

1. Add ingredients to the bread machine following the manufacturer's guidelines.
2. Choose the sweet bread setting and start the machine.
3. Once the dough is ready, mix brown sugar and cinnamon in a bowl.
4. Cut the dough into small pieces and roll them in the sugar-cinnamon mixture.
5. Layer the pieces in a greased bundt pan, adding chopped pecans between the layers.
6. Pour caramel sauce over the top, let it rise for 30 minutes, then bake in a preheated oven at 350°F (180°C) for 30-35 minutes or until golden.
7. Cool the caramel pecan monkey bread in the pan for 10 minutes, then invert onto a serving plate.

Nutritional Value (per serving):

- Calories: 220
- Protein: 5g
- Carbohydrates: 35g
- Fat: 6g
- Fiber: 2g

Gingerbread Loaf with Cream Cheese Swirl

Prep Time: 25 minutes
Cook Time: 3 hours
Serving Size: 1 loaf

Ingredients:

- 2 1/2 cups bread flour
- 1/2 cup whole wheat flour

- 1 1/2 teaspoons salt
- 1 1/4 cups warm water
- 1/2 cup molasses
- 2 tablespoons unsalted butter, melted
- 1 teaspoon ground ginger
- 1 teaspoon ground cinnamon
- 1/2 teaspoon ground cloves
- 1/4 teaspoon nutmeg
- 2 teaspoons active dry yeast
- Cream Cheese Swirl:
    - 4 oz cream cheese, softened
    - 1/4 cup powdered sugar
    - 1 egg

Instructions:

1. Add bread ingredients to the bread machine following the manufacturer's guidelines.
2. Choose the sweet bread setting and start the machine.
3. Once the dough is ready, roll it out on a floured surface.
4. In a separate bowl, mix softened cream cheese, powdered sugar, and egg to create the cream cheese swirl.
5. Spread the cream cheese mixture over the rolled-out dough, then roll it into a log and place it in a greased loaf pan.
6. Let it rise for 30 minutes, then bake the gingerbread loaf in a preheated oven at 375°F (190°C) for 35-40 minutes or until a toothpick comes out clean.
7. Cool the bread on a wire rack before slicing.

Nutritional Value (per serving):

- Calories: 200
- Protein: 4g
- Carbohydrates: 35g
- Fat: 5g
- Fiber: 2g

Cherry Almond Brioche Wreath

Prep Time: 30 minutes
Cook Time: 3 hours
Serving Size: 1 wreath

Ingredients:

- 3 cups bread flour
- 1/4 cup sugar
- 1 1/2 teaspoons salt
- 1/2 cup warm milk
- 3 tablespoons unsalted butter, melted
- 3 large eggs
- 1/2 cup chopped almonds
- 1/2 cup dried cherries
- 2 teaspoons almond extract
- 2 teaspoons active dry yeast
- Icing:
    - 1 cup powdered sugar

- 2 tablespoons milk
- 1/2 teaspoon almond extract

Instructions:

1. Add bread ingredients to the bread machine following the manufacturer's guidelines.
2. Choose the sweet bread setting and start the machine.
3. Once the dough is ready, fold in chopped almonds, dried cherries, and almond extract.
4. Transfer the dough to a floured surface and shape it into a wreath.
5. Place the wreath on a parchment-lined baking sheet, let it rise for 30 minutes, then bake in a preheated oven at 350°F (180°C) for 25-30 minutes or until golden.
6. In a bowl, mix powdered sugar, milk, and almond extract to create the icing. Drizzle over the cooled brioche wreath.

Nutritional Value (per serving):

- Calories: 220
- Protein: 5g
- Carbohydrates: 35g
- Fat: 6g
- Fiber: 2g

Orange Cranberry Babka

Prep Time: 35 minutes
Cook Time: 3 hours
Serving Size: 1 babka

Ingredients:

- 3 cups bread flour
- 1/4 cup sugar
- 1 1/2 teaspoons salt
- 1/2 cup warm milk
- 3 tablespoons unsalted butter, melted
- 3 large eggs
- Zest of one orange
- 1/2 cup dried cranberries
- 2 teaspoons active dry yeast
- Filling:
    - 1/2 cup sugar
    - 1 tablespoon ground cinnamon
    - 1/4 cup unsalted butter, melted

Instructions:

1. Add bread ingredients to the bread machine following the manufacturer's guidelines.
2. Choose the sweet bread setting and start the machine.
3. Once the dough is ready, roll it out on a floured surface.
4. Mix sugar, cinnamon, and melted butter to create the filling. Spread it over the rolled-out dough, then sprinkle dried cranberries and orange zest.

5. Roll the dough into a log and cut it in half lengthwise. Twist the two halves together and place the twisted dough in a greased loaf pan.

6. Let it rise for 30 minutes, then bake the orange cranberry babka in a preheated oven at 375°F (190°C) for 35-40 minutes or until a toothpick comes out clean.

7. Cool the bread on a wire rack before slicing.

Nutritional Value (per serving):

- Calories: 210
- Protein: 4g
- Carbohydrates: 35g
- Fat: 5g
- Fiber: 2g

Cinnamon Roll Swirl Bread with Cream Cheese Glaze

Prep Time: 30 minutes
Cook Time: 3 hours
Serving Size: 1 loaf

Ingredients:

- 2 1/2 cups bread flour
- 1/4 cup sugar
- 1 1/2 teaspoons salt
- 1 cup warm milk
- 3 tablespoons unsalted butter, melted
- 2 teaspoons ground cinnamon
- 1/4 cup brown sugar

- 2 teaspoons active dry yeast
- Cream Cheese Glaze:
    - 4 oz cream cheese, softened
    - 1/2 cup powdered sugar
    - 2 tablespoons milk
    - 1 teaspoon vanilla extract

Instructions:

1. Add bread ingredients to the bread machine following the manufacturer's guidelines.
2. Choose the sweet bread or cinnamon roll setting and start the machine.
3. Once the dough is ready, roll it out on a floured surface.
4. Mix ground cinnamon and brown sugar, then spread it over the rolled-out dough.
5. Roll the dough into a log and place it in a greased loaf pan. Let it rise for 30 minutes.
6. Bake the cinnamon roll swirl bread in a preheated oven at 375°F (190°C) for 35-40 minutes or until a toothpick comes out clean.
7. Mix cream cheese, powdered sugar, milk, and vanilla extract to create the glaze. Drizzle over the cooled bread.

Nutritional Value (per serving):

- Calories: 220
- Protein: 5g
- Carbohydrates: 35g
- Fat: 6g
- Fiber: 2g

Chocolate Orange Braided Bread

Prep Time: 35 minutes
Cook Time: 3 hours
Serving Size: 1 braided loaf

Ingredients:

- 3 cups bread flour
- 1/4 cup sugar
- 1 1/2 teaspoons salt
- 1/2 cup warm water
- 1/4 cup orange juice
- 3 tablespoons unsalted butter, melted
- 2 teaspoons orange zest
- 1/4 cup cocoa powder
- 2 tablespoons sugar
- 2 teaspoons active dry yeast
- 1 egg (for egg wash)
- Orange glaze:
    - 1 cup powdered sugar
    - 2 tablespoons orange juice
    - Orange zest for garnish

Instructions:

1. Add bread ingredients (except cocoa powder and additional sugar) to the bread machine following the manufacturer's guidelines.
2. Choose the sweet bread or braid setting and start the machine.

3. Once the dough is ready, divide it in half. To one half, add cocoa powder and sugar, mix well.

4. Roll each portion into ropes, then braid the ropes together and place the braided dough in a greased loaf pan. Let it rise for 30 minutes.

5. Brush the braided bread with egg wash and bake in a preheated oven at 350°F (180°C) for 30-35 minutes or until golden brown.

6. Mix powdered sugar and orange juice to create the glaze. Drizzle over the cooled bread and garnish with orange zest.

Nutritional Value (per serving):

- Calories: 230
- Protein: 5g
- Carbohydrates: 40g
- Fat: 6g
- Fiber: 2g

Hazelnut Praline Twist Bread

Prep Time: 25 minutes
Cook Time: 3 hours
Serving Size: 1 twist loaf

Ingredients:

- 3 cups bread flour
- 1/4 cup sugar
- 1 1/2 teaspoons salt
- 1/2 cup warm milk
- 3 tablespoons unsalted butter, melted

- 1/2 cup hazelnuts, toasted and chopped
- 1/4 cup brown sugar
- 2 teaspoons ground cinnamon
- 2 teaspoons active dry yeast
- Glaze:
    - 1/2 cup powdered sugar
    - 2 tablespoons milk
    - Chopped hazelnuts for garnish

Instructions:

1. Add bread ingredients to the bread machine following the manufacturer's guidelines.
2. Choose the sweet bread or twist setting and start the machine.
3. Once the dough is ready, roll it out on a floured surface.
4. Mix toasted hazelnuts, brown sugar, and cinnamon. Spread the mixture over the rolled-out dough.
5. Roll the dough into a log, then twist it into a loaf shape and place it in a greased pan. Let it rise for 30 minutes.
6. Bake the hazelnut praline twist bread in a preheated oven at 375°F (190°C) for 35-40 minutes or until a toothpick comes out clean.
7. Mix powdered sugar and milk to create the glaze. Drizzle over the cooled bread and garnish with chopped hazelnuts.

Nutritional Value (per serving):

- Calories: 240
- Protein: 6g
- Carbohydrates: 35g

- Fat: 7g
- Fiber: 2.5g

Chapter Seven

Jam and Nut Dispenser Recipes

Strawberry Almond Jam Swirl Bread

Prep Time: 25 minutes
Cook Time: 3 hours
Serving Size: 1 loaf

Ingredients:

- 2 1/2 cups bread flour
- 1/4 cup sugar
- 1 1/2 teaspoons salt
- 1 cup warm water
- 2 tablespoons unsalted butter, melted
- 1/2 cup strawberry jam
- 1/2 cup sliced almonds
- 2 teaspoons active dry yeast

Instructions:

1. Add ingredients (except jam and almonds) to the bread machine following the manufacturer's guidelines.
2. Choose the sweet bread or swirl setting and start the machine.
3. Once the dough is ready, roll it out on a floured surface.
4. Spread strawberry jam over the rolled-out dough and sprinkle sliced almonds.
5. Roll the dough into a log and place it in a greased loaf pan. Let it rise for 30 minutes.
6. Bake the strawberry almond jam swirl bread in a preheated oven at 375°F (190°C) for 35-40 minutes or until a toothpick comes out clean.

7. Cool the bread on a wire rack before slicing.

Nutritional Value (per serving):

- Calories: 220
- Protein: 5g
- Carbohydrates: 35g
- Fat: 6g
- Fiber: 2g

Apricot Walnut Dispenser Bread

Prep Time: 20 minutes
Cook Time: 3 hours
Serving Size: 1 loaf

Ingredients:

- 3 cups bread flour
- 1/4 cup sugar
- 1 1/2 teaspoons salt
- 1 cup warm milk
- 3 tablespoons unsalted butter, melted
- 1/2 cup apricot preserves
- 1/2 cup chopped walnuts
- 2 teaspoons active dry yeast

Instructions:

1. Add ingredients (except apricot preserves and walnuts) to the bread machine following the manufacturer's guidelines.

2. Choose the sweet bread or nut dispenser setting and start the machine.

3. Once the dough is ready, fold in chopped walnuts.

4. Transfer the dough to a greased loaf pan and let it rise for 30 minutes.

5. Bake the apricot walnut dispenser bread in a preheated oven at 350°F (180°C) for 35-40 minutes or until a toothpick comes out clean.

6. Cool the bread on a wire rack before slicing.

Nutritional Value (per serving):

- Calories: 210
- Protein: 4g
- Carbohydrates: 35g
- Fat: 5g
- Fiber: 2g

Raspberry Hazelnut Swirl Loaf

Prep Time: 30 minutes
Cook Time: 3 hours
Serving Size: 1 loaf

Ingredients:

- 2 1/2 cups bread flour
- 1/4 cup sugar
- 1 1/2 teaspoons salt
- 1 cup warm water
- 2 tablespoons unsalted butter, melted
- 1/2 cup raspberry jam

- 1/2 cup chopped hazelnuts
- 2 teaspoons active dry yeast

Instructions:

1. Add ingredients (except jam and hazelnuts) to the bread machine following the manufacturer's guidelines.
2. Choose the sweet bread or swirl setting and start the machine.
3. Once the dough is ready, roll it out on a floured surface.
4. Spread raspberry jam over the rolled-out dough and sprinkle chopped hazelnuts.
5. Roll the dough into a log and place it in a greased loaf pan. Let it rise for 30 minutes.
6. Bake the raspberry hazelnut swirl loaf in a preheated oven at 375°F (190°C) for 35-40 minutes or until a toothpick comes out clean.
7. Cool the bread on a wire rack before slicing.

Nutritional Value (per serving):

- Calories: 230
- Protein: 5g
- Carbohydrates: 35g
- Fat: 6g
- Fiber: 2.5g

Blueberry Pecan Burst Bread

Prep Time: 25 minutes
Cook Time: 3 hours
Serving Size: 1 loaf

Ingredients:

- 3 cups bread flour
- 1/4 cup sugar
- 1 1/2 teaspoons salt
- 1/2 cup warm water
- 1/4 cup olive oil
- 1/2 cup blueberry jam
- 1/2 cup chopped pecans
- 2 teaspoons active dry yeast

Instructions:

1. Add ingredients (except jam and pecans) to the bread machine following the manufacturer's guidelines.
2. Choose the sweet bread or nut dispenser setting and start the machine.
3. Once the dough is ready, fold in chopped pecans.
4. Transfer the dough to a greased loaf pan and create a well in the center.
5. Spoon blueberry jam into the well, covering it with dough. Let it rise for 30 minutes.
6. Bake the blueberry pecan burst bread in a preheated oven at 350°F (180°C) for 35-40 minutes or until a toothpick comes out clean.
7. Cool the bread on a wire rack before slicing.

Nutritional Value (per serving):

- Calories: 220
- Protein: 4.5g
- Carbohydrates: 35g
- Fat: 6g
- Fiber: 2g

Cherry Chocolate Nut Delight

Prep Time: 30 minutes
Cook Time: 3 hours
Serving Size: 1 loaf

Ingredients:

- 2 1/2 cups bread flour
- 1/4 cup sugar
- 1 1/2 teaspoons salt
- 1 cup warm milk
- 3 tablespoons unsalted butter, melted
- 1/2 cup cherry jam
- 1/2 cup chopped mixed nuts (almonds, walnuts, and hazelnuts)
- 1/4 cup chocolate chips
- 2 teaspoons active dry yeast

Instructions:

1. Add ingredients (except jam, nuts, and chocolate chips) to the bread machine following the manufacturer's guidelines.
2. Choose the sweet bread or nut dispenser setting and start the machine.

3. Once the dough is ready, fold in chopped mixed nuts and chocolate chips.

4. Transfer the dough to a greased loaf pan and make a swirl in the center.

5. Spoon cherry jam into the swirl. Let it rise for 30 minutes.

6. Bake the cherry chocolate nut delight bread in a preheated oven at 375°F (190°C) for 35-40 minutes or until a toothpick comes out clean.

7. Cool the bread on a wire rack before slicing.

Nutritional Value (per serving):

- Calories: 230
- Protein: 5g
- Carbohydrates: 35g
- Fat: 6g
- Fiber: 2g

Peach Pecan Bliss Bread

Prep Time: 25 minutes
Cook Time: 3 hours
Serving Size: 1 loaf

Ingredients:

- 3 cups bread flour
- 1/4 cup sugar
- 1 1/2 teaspoons salt
- 1/2 cup warm water
- 1/4 cup olive oil
- 1/2 cup peach preserves

- 1/2 cup chopped pecans
- 2 teaspoons active dry yeast

Instructions:

1. Add ingredients (except peach preserves and pecans) to the bread machine following the manufacturer's guidelines.
2. Choose the sweet bread or nut dispenser setting and start the machine.
3. Once the dough is ready, fold in chopped pecans.
4. Transfer the dough to a greased loaf pan and create a well in the center.
5. Spoon peach preserves into the well, covering it with dough. Let it rise for 30 minutes.
6. Bake the peach pecan bliss bread in a preheated oven at 350°F (180°C) for 35-40 minutes or until a toothpick comes out clean.
7. Cool the bread on a wire rack before slicing.

Nutritional Value (per serving):

- Calories: 220
- Protein: 4.5g
- Carbohydrates: 35g
- Fat: 6g
- Fiber: 2g

Raspberry Almond Crunch Bread

Prep Time: 30 minutes
Cook Time: 3 hours
Serving Size: 1 loaf

Ingredients:

- 2 1/2 cups bread flour
- 1/4 cup sugar
- 1 1/2 teaspoons salt
- 1 cup warm water
- 2 tablespoons unsalted butter, melted
- 1/2 cup raspberry jam
- 1/2 cup sliced almonds
- 1/4 cup granola
- 2 teaspoons active dry yeast

Instructions:

1. Add ingredients (except jam, almonds, and granola) to the bread machine following the manufacturer's guidelines.
2. Choose the sweet bread or nut dispenser setting and start the machine.
3. Once the dough is ready, spread raspberry jam over the surface and sprinkle sliced almonds and granola.
4. Roll the dough into a log and place it in a greased loaf pan. Let it rise for 30 minutes.
5. Bake the raspberry almond crunch bread in a preheated oven at 375°F (190°C) for 35-40 minutes or until a toothpick comes out clean.
6. Cool the bread on a wire rack before slicing.

Nutritional Value (per serving):

- Calories: 230
- Protein: 5g
- Carbohydrates: 35g
- Fat: 6g
- Fiber: 2g

Blackberry Walnut Surprise Loaf

Prep Time: 25 minutes
Cook Time: 3 hours
Serving Size: 1 loaf

Ingredients:

- 3 cups bread flour
- 1/4 cup sugar
- 1 1/2 teaspoons salt
- 1 cup warm milk
- 3 tablespoons unsalted butter, melted
- 1/2 cup blackberry jam
- 1/2 cup chopped walnuts
- 2 teaspoons active dry yeast

Instructions:

1. Add ingredients (except jam and walnuts) to the bread machine following the manufacturer's guidelines.
2. Choose the sweet bread or nut dispenser setting and start the machine.
3. Once the dough is ready, fold in chopped walnuts.
4. Transfer the dough to a greased loaf pan and make a well in the center.

5. Spoon blackberry jam into the well. Let it rise for 30 minutes.
6. Bake the blackberry walnut surprise loaf in a preheated oven at 350°F (180°C) for 35-40 minutes or until a toothpick comes out clean.
7. Cool the bread on a wire rack before slicing.

Nutritional Value (per serving):

- Calories: 220
- Protein: 4g
- Carbohydrates: 35g
- Fat: 5g
- Fiber: 2g

Apple Cinnamon Pecan Delight Bread

Prep Time: 30 minutes
Cook Time: 3 hours
Serving Size: 1 loaf

Ingredients:

- 2 1/2 cups bread flour
- 1/4 cup sugar
- 1 1/2 teaspoons salt
- 1 cup warm water
- 2 tablespoons unsalted butter, melted
- 1/2 cup apple jam or applesauce
- 1/2 cup chopped pecans
- 2 teaspoons ground cinnamon

- 2 teaspoons active dry yeast

Instructions:

1. Add ingredients (except jam, pecans, and cinnamon) to the bread machine following the manufacturer's guidelines.
2. Choose the sweet bread or nut dispenser setting and start the machine.
3. Once the dough is ready, fold in chopped pecans and sprinkle ground cinnamon.
4. Transfer the dough to a greased loaf pan and make a well in the center.
5. Spoon apple jam or applesauce into the well. Let it rise for 30 minutes.
6. Bake the apple cinnamon pecan delight bread in a preheated oven at 375°F (190°C) for 35-40 minutes or until a toothpick comes out clean.
7. Cool the bread on a wire rack before slicing.

Nutritional Value (per serving):

- Calories: 240
- Protein: 6g
- Carbohydrates: 35g
- Fat: 7g
- Fiber: 2.5g

Fig and Pistachio Swirl Bread

Prep Time: 35 minutes
Cook Time: 3 hours
Serving Size: 1 loaf

Ingredients:

- 3 cups bread flour

- 1/4 cup sugar
- 1 1/2 teaspoons salt
- 1/2 cup warm water
- 1/4 cup olive oil
- 1/2 cup fig jam
- 1/2 cup chopped pistachios
- 2 teaspoons active dry yeast

Instructions:

1. Add ingredients (except jam and pistachios) to the bread machine following the manufacturer's guidelines.
2. Choose the sweet bread or nut dispenser setting and start the machine.
3. Once the dough is ready, spread fig jam over the surface and sprinkle chopped pistachios.
4. Roll the dough into a log and place it in a greased loaf pan. Let it rise for 30 minutes.
5. Bake the fig and pistachio swirl bread in a preheated oven at 375°F (190°C) for 35-40 minutes or until a toothpick comes out clean.
6. Cool the bread on a wire rack before slicing.

Nutritional Value (per serving):

- Calories: 240
- Protein: 6g
- Carbohydrates: 35g
- Fat: 7g
- Fiber: 2.5g

Cranberry Orange Walnut Bliss

Prep Time: 30 minutes
Cook Time: 3 hours
Serving Size: 1 loaf

Ingredients:

- 2 1/2 cups bread flour
- 1/4 cup sugar
- 1 1/2 teaspoons salt
- 1 cup warm water
- 2 tablespoons unsalted butter, melted
- 1/2 cup cranberry jam or whole cranberry sauce
- 1/2 cup chopped walnuts
- Zest of one orange
- 2 teaspoons active dry yeast

Instructions:

1. Add ingredients (except jam, walnuts, and orange zest) to the bread machine following the manufacturer's guidelines.
2. Choose the sweet bread or nut dispenser setting and start the machine.
3. Once the dough is ready, fold in chopped walnuts and orange zest.
4. Transfer the dough to a greased loaf pan and create a well in the center.
5. Spoon cranberry jam or whole cranberry sauce into the well. Let it rise for 30 minutes.
6. Bake the cranberry orange walnut bliss bread in a preheated oven at 350°F (180°C) for 35-40 minutes or until a toothpick comes out clean.
7. Cool the bread on a wire rack before slicing.

Nutritional Value (per serving):

- Calories: 230
- Protein: 5g
- Carbohydrates: 35g
- Fat: 6g
- Fiber: 2g

Mango Coconut Macadamia Bread

Prep Time: 35 minutes
Cook Time: 3 hours
Serving Size: 1 loaf

Ingredients:

- 3 cups bread flour
- 1/4 cup sugar
- 1 1/2 teaspoons salt
- 1/2 cup warm water
- 1/4 cup coconut oil
- 1/2 cup mango jam or puree
- 1/2 cup chopped macadamia nuts
- 2 teaspoons active dry yeast

Instructions:

1. Add ingredients (except jam and macadamia nuts) to the bread machine following the manufacturer's guidelines.
2. Choose the sweet bread or nut dispenser setting and start the machine.

3. Once the dough is ready, fold in chopped macadamia nuts.
4. Transfer the dough to a greased loaf pan and make a swirl in the center.
5. Spoon mango jam or puree into the swirl. Let it rise for 30 minutes.
6. Bake the mango coconut macadamia bread in a preheated oven at 375°F (190°C) for 35-40 minutes or until a toothpick comes out clean.
7. Cool the bread on a wire rack before slicing.

Nutritional Value (per serving):

- Calories: 240
- Protein: 6g
- Carbohydrates: 35g
- Fat: 7g
- Fiber: 2.5g

Pomegranate Pistachio Delight

Prep Time: 30 minutes
Cook Time: 3 hours
Serving Size: 1 loaf

Ingredients:

- 2 1/2 cups bread flour
- 1/4 cup sugar
- 1 1/2 teaspoons salt
- 1 cup warm water
- 2 tablespoons olive oil
- 1/2 cup pomegranate jam or molasses

- 1/2 cup chopped pistachios
- 2 teaspoons active dry yeast

Instructions:

1. Add ingredients (except jam and pistachios) to the bread machine following the manufacturer's guidelines.
2. Choose the sweet bread or nut dispenser setting and start the machine.
3. Once the dough is ready, spread pomegranate jam or molasses over the surface and sprinkle chopped pistachios.
4. Roll the dough into a log and place it in a greased loaf pan. Let it rise for 30 minutes.
5. Bake the pomegranate pistachio delight bread in a preheated oven at 375°F (190°C) for 35-40 minutes or until a toothpick comes out clean.
6. Cool the bread on a wire rack before slicing.

Nutritional Value (per serving):

- Calories: 240
- Protein: 6g
- Carbohydrates: 35g
- Fat: 7g
- Fiber: 2.5g

Pear Ginger Walnut Swirl Bread

Prep Time: 35 minutes
Cook Time: 3 hours
Serving Size: 1 loaf

Ingredients:

- 3 cups bread flour

- 1/4 cup sugar
- 1 1/2 teaspoons salt
- 1/2 cup warm milk
- 3 tablespoons unsalted butter, melted
- 1/2 cup pear preserves or puree
- 1/2 cup chopped walnuts
- 1 teaspoon ground ginger
- 2 teaspoons active dry yeast

Instructions:

1. Add ingredients (except pear preserves, walnuts, and ground ginger) to the bread machine following the manufacturer's guidelines.
2. Choose the sweet bread or nut dispenser setting and start the machine.
3. Once the dough is ready, fold in chopped walnuts and ground ginger.
4. Transfer the dough to a greased loaf pan and create a well in the center.
5. Spoon pear preserves or puree into the well. Let it rise for 30 minutes.
6. Bake the pear ginger walnut swirl bread in a preheated oven at 350°F (180°C) for 35-40 minutes or until a toothpick comes out clean.
7. Cool the bread on a wire rack before slicing.

Nutritional Value (per serving):

- Calories: 230
- Protein: 5g
- Carbohydrates: 35g
- Fat: 6g

- Fiber: 2g

Cherry Pistachio Coconut Loaf

Prep Time: 30 minutes
Cook Time: 3 hours
Serving Size: 1 loaf

Ingredients:

- 2 1/2 cups bread flour
- 1/4 cup sugar
- 1 1/2 teaspoons salt
- 1 cup warm water
- 2 tablespoons coconut oil
- 1/2 cup cherry jam
- 1/2 cup chopped pistachios
- 1/4 cup shredded coconut
- 2 teaspoons active dry yeast

Instructions:

1. Add ingredients (except jam, pistachios, and shredded coconut) to the bread machine following the manufacturer's guidelines.
2. Choose the sweet bread or nut dispenser setting and start the machine.
3. Once the dough is ready, fold in chopped pistachios and shredded coconut.
4. Transfer the dough to a greased loaf pan and make a swirl in the center.
5. Spoon cherry jam into the swirl. Let it rise for 30 minutes.

6. Bake the cherry pistachio coconut loaf in a preheated oven at 375°F (190°C) for 35-40 minutes or until a toothpick comes out clean.

7. Cool the bread on a wire rack before slicing.

Nutritional Value (per serving):

- Calories: 240
- Protein: 6g
- Carbohydrates: 35g
- Fat: 7g
- Fiber: 2.5g

Chapter Eight

Dough-Only Recipes

Classic Pizza Dough

Prep Time: 10 minutes
Cook Time: N/A
Serving Size: 1 pizza crust

Ingredients:

- 3 cups bread flour
- 1 teaspoon sugar
- 1 1/2 teaspoons salt
- 1 tablespoon olive oil
- 1 1/4 cups warm water
- 2 teaspoons active dry yeast

Instructions:

1. Add ingredients to the bread machine following the manufacturer's guidelines for dough.
2. Choose the dough setting and start the machine.
3. Once the dough is ready, remove and roll it out on a floured surface to desired pizza crust thickness.
4. Add your favorite pizza toppings.
5. Bake in a preheated oven according to your pizza recipe.

Nutritional Value (per serving):

- Calories: 160
- Protein: 4g

- Carbohydrates: 30g
- Fat: 2g
- Fiber: 1g

Soft Pretzel Dough

Prep Time: 15 minutes
Cook Time: N/A
Serving Size: 8 pretzels

Ingredients:

- 3 1/2 cups all-purpose flour
- 1/4 cup sugar
- 1 teaspoon salt
- 1 1/4 cups warm water
- 2 tablespoons unsalted butter, melted
- 2 teaspoons active dry yeast
- 10 cups water
- 2/3 cup baking soda
- Coarse salt for topping

Instructions:

1. Add flour, sugar, salt, warm water, melted butter, and yeast to the bread machine following the manufacturer's guidelines for dough.
2. Choose the dough setting and start the machine.
3. Once the dough is ready, preheat the oven to 425°F (220°C).
4. Divide the dough into 8 portions and roll each into a rope.

5. In a large pot, bring 10 cups of water to a boil. Add baking soda.

6. Boil each pretzel for 30 seconds, then place on a baking sheet.

7. Sprinkle with coarse salt and bake for 12-15 minutes or until golden brown.

Nutritional Value (per serving):

- Calories: 250
- Protein: 6g
- Carbohydrates: 50g
- Fat: 3g
- Fiber: 2g

Garlic Herb Breadsticks Dough

Prep Time: 15 minutes
Cook Time: N/A
Serving Size: 12 breadsticks

Ingredients:

- 3 cups bread flour
- 1 tablespoon sugar
- 1 1/2 teaspoons salt
- 1 tablespoon olive oil
- 1 1/4 cups warm water
- 2 teaspoons active dry yeast
- 3 tablespoons unsalted butter, melted
- 2 cloves garlic, minced
- 1 teaspoon dried parsley

- 1/2 teaspoon dried oregano

Instructions:

1. Add flour, sugar, salt, olive oil, warm water, and yeast to the bread machine following the manufacturer's guidelines for dough.
2. Choose the dough setting and start the machine.
3. Once the dough is ready, preheat the oven to 375°F (190°C).
4. Roll out the dough into a rectangle on a floured surface.
5. Mix melted butter, minced garlic, dried parsley, and dried oregano. Spread over the dough.
6. Cut the dough into 12 strips and twist each strip.
7. Place on a baking sheet and bake for 12-15 minutes or until golden brown.

Nutritional Value (per serving):

- Calories: 160
- Protein: 4g
- Carbohydrates: 25g
- Fat: 5g
- Fiber: 1g

Cinnamon Roll Dough

Prep Time: 20 minutes
Cook Time: N/A
Serving Size: 12 cinnamon rolls

Ingredients:

- 3 1/2 cups all-purpose flour

- 1/4 cup sugar
- 1 teaspoon salt
- 1 1/4 cups warm milk
- 3 tablespoons unsalted butter, melted
- 2 teaspoons active dry yeast
- 1/3 cup brown sugar
- 1 tablespoon ground cinnamon
- Cream cheese frosting for topping

Instructions:

1. Add flour, sugar, salt, warm milk, melted butter, and yeast to the bread machine following the manufacturer's guidelines for dough.
2. Choose the dough setting and start the machine.
3. Once the dough is ready, preheat the oven to 375°F (190°C).
4. Roll out the dough into a rectangle on a floured surface.
5. Mix brown sugar and ground cinnamon. Spread over the dough.
6. Roll the dough into a log and cut into 12 slices.
7. Place on a greased baking pan and bake for 15-18 minutes.
8. Drizzle with cream cheese frosting.

Nutritional Value (per serving):

- Calories: 280
- Protein: 4g
- Carbohydrates: 45g
- Fat: 8g

- Fiber: 2g

Herb Focaccia Dough

Prep Time: 15 minutes
Cook Time: N/A
Serving Size: 1 focaccia bread

Ingredients:

- 3 1/2 cups bread flour
- 1 teaspoon sugar
- 1 1/2 teaspoons salt
- 1 tablespoon olive oil
- 1 1/4 cups warm water
- 2 teaspoons active dry yeast
- 2 tablespoons olive oil (for topping)
- 1 teaspoon dried rosemary
- 1 teaspoon dried thyme
- Coarse sea salt for sprinkling

Instructions:

1. Add flour, sugar, salt, olive oil, warm water, and yeast to the bread machine following the manufacturer's guidelines for dough.
2. Choose the dough setting and start the machine.
3. Once the dough is ready, preheat the oven to 400°F (200°C).
4. Roll out the dough onto a baking sheet.
5. Press dimples into the dough with your fingers.

6. Drizzle with olive oil, sprinkle with dried rosemary, dried thyme, and coarse sea salt.

7. Let it rise for 20 minutes.

8. Bake for 20-25 minutes or until golden brown.

Nutritional Value (per serving):

- Calories: 210
- Protein: 5g
- Carbohydrates: 35g
- Fat: 6g
- Fiber: 2g

Bagel Dough

Prep Time: 20 minutes
Cook Time: N/A
Serving Size: 8 bagels

Ingredients:

- 4 cups bread flour
- 1 tablespoon sugar
- 1 1/2 teaspoons salt
- 1 1/4 cups warm water
- 2 teaspoons active dry yeast
- 1 egg, beaten (for egg wash)
- Sesame seeds or poppy seeds for topping

Instructions:

1. Add flour, sugar, salt, warm water, and yeast to the bread machine following the manufacturer's guidelines for dough.
2. Choose the dough setting and start the machine.
3. Once the dough is ready, preheat the oven to 425°F (220°C).
4. Divide the dough into 8 portions and shape each into a bagel.
5. Place on a parchment-lined baking sheet.
6. Let them rise for 20 minutes.
7. Brush with beaten egg and sprinkle with sesame seeds or poppy seeds.
8. Bake for 15-18 minutes or until golden brown.

Nutritional Value (per serving):

- Calories: 240
- Protein: 7g
- Carbohydrates: 45g
- Fat: 2g
- Fiber: 2g

Whole Wheat Bread Dough

Prep Time: 15 minutes
Cook Time: N/A
Serving Size: 1 loaf

Ingredients:

- 2 1/2 cups whole wheat flour
- 1 1/2 cups bread flour
- 1 tablespoon sugar

- 1 1/2 teaspoons salt
- 1 1/4 cups warm water
- 2 tablespoons olive oil
- 2 teaspoons active dry yeast

Instructions:

1. Add whole wheat flour, bread flour, sugar, salt, olive oil, warm water, and yeast to the bread machine following the manufacturer's guidelines for dough.
2. Choose the dough setting and start the machine.
3. Once the dough is ready, preheat the oven to 350°F (180°C).
4. Shape the dough into a loaf and place it in a greased loaf pan.
5. Let it rise for 30 minutes.
6. Bake for 25-30 minutes or until the top is golden brown.

Nutritional Value (per serving):

- Calories: 190
- Protein: 6g
- Carbohydrates: 36g
- Fat: 3.5g
- Fiber: 5g

Pita Bread Dough

Prep Time: 15 minutes
Cook Time: N/A
Serving Size: 8 pita breads

Ingredients:

- 3 cups bread flour
- 1 teaspoon sugar
- 1 1/2 teaspoons salt
- 1 tablespoon olive oil
- 1 1/4 cups warm water
- 2 teaspoons active dry yeast

Instructions:

1. Add flour, sugar, salt, olive oil, warm water, and yeast to the bread machine following the manufacturer's guidelines for dough.
2. Choose the dough setting and start the machine.
3. Once the dough is ready, preheat the oven to 450°F (230°C).
4. Divide the dough into 8 portions and roll each into a ball.
5. Roll out each ball into a flat circle.
6. Place on a baking sheet and let them rise for 15 minutes.
7. Bake for 8-10 minutes or until puffed and lightly browned.

Nutritional Value (per serving):

- Calories: 150
- Protein: 4g
- Carbohydrates: 30g

- Fat: 2g
- Fiber: 1g

These dough-only recipes provide a versatile foundation for various baked goods, from cinnamon rolls to bagels. Customize and enjoy these homemade creations fresh from your bread machine!

Brioche Dough

Prep Time: 20 minutes
Cook Time: N/A
Serving Size: 1 loaf

Ingredients:

- 3 cups bread flour
- 1/4 cup sugar
- 1 1/2 teaspoons salt
- 1/2 cup unsalted butter, softened
- 1/2 cup warm milk
- 3 large eggs
- 2 teaspoons active dry yeast

Instructions:

1. Add flour, sugar, salt, softened butter, warm milk, eggs, and yeast to the bread machine following the manufacturer's guidelines for dough.
2. Choose the dough setting and start the machine.
3. Once the dough is ready, preheat the oven to 375°F (190°C).
4. Shape the dough into a loaf and place it in a greased loaf pan.

5. Let it rise for 30-45 minutes.
6. Bake for 25-30 minutes or until golden brown.

Nutritional Value (per serving):

- Calories: 280
- Protein: 7g
- Carbohydrates: 35g
- Fat: 12g
- Fiber: 1g

Olive and Rosemary Fougasse Dough

Prep Time: 25 minutes
Cook Time: N/A
Serving Size: 1 fougasse

Ingredients:

- 3 cups bread flour
- 1 1/2 teaspoons salt
- 1 1/4 cups warm water
- 2 tablespoons olive oil
- 1/2 cup pitted green olives, chopped
- 1 tablespoon fresh rosemary, chopped
- 2 teaspoons active dry yeast

Instructions:

1. Add flour, salt, warm water, olive oil, olives, rosemary, and yeast to the bread machine following the manufacturer's guidelines for dough.

2. Choose the dough setting and start the machine.
3. Once the dough is ready, preheat the oven to 425°F (220°C).
4. Roll out the dough into a free-form oval shape.
5. Make several cuts in the dough to resemble leaf veins.
6. Bake for 20-25 minutes or until golden brown.

Nutritional Value (per serving):

- Calories: 230
- Protein: 5g
- Carbohydrates: 35g
- Fat: 6g
- Fiber: 2g

Sourdough Bread Dough

Prep Time: 15 minutes (plus sourdough fermentation time)
Cook Time: N/A
Serving Size: 1 loaf

Ingredients:

- 3 cups bread flour
- 1 1/2 teaspoons salt
- 1 1/4 cups warm water
- 1/2 cup active sourdough starter
- 2 teaspoons honey
- 2 teaspoons olive oil

Instructions:

1. Add flour, salt, warm water, sourdough starter, honey, and olive oil to the bread machine following the manufacturer's guidelines for dough.
2. Choose the dough setting and start the machine.
3. Once the dough is ready, preheat the oven to 425°F (220°C).
4. Shape the dough into a round loaf and place it on a baking sheet.
5. Let it rise for 1-2 hours.
6. Bake for 25-30 minutes or until the crust is golden brown.

Nutritional Value (per serving):

- Calories: 240
- Protein: 6g
- Carbohydrates: 45g
- Fat: 3g
- Fiber: 2g

Sun-Dried Tomato and Basil Bread Dough

Prep Time: 20 minutes
Cook Time: N/A
Serving Size: 1 loaf

Ingredients:

- 3 cups bread flour
- 1 1/2 teaspoons salt
- 1 1/4 cups warm water
- 2 tablespoons olive oil
- 1/2 cup sun-dried tomatoes, chopped

- 1/4 cup fresh basil, chopped
- 2 teaspoons active dry yeast

Instructions:

1. Add flour, salt, warm water, olive oil, sun-dried tomatoes, basil, and yeast to the bread machine following the manufacturer's guidelines for dough.
2. Choose the dough setting and start the machine.
3. Once the dough is ready, preheat the oven to 375°F (190°C).
4. Shape the dough into a round or oval loaf and place it in a greased loaf pan.
5. Let it rise for 30-45 minutes.
6. Bake for 25-30 minutes or until the top is golden brown.

Nutritional Value (per serving):

- Calories: 260
- Protein: 7g
- Carbohydrates: 45g
- Fat: 5g
- Fiber: 2g

Cranberry Walnut Bread Dough

Prep Time: 20 minutes
Cook Time: N/A
Serving Size: 1 loaf

Ingredients:

- 3 cups bread flour
- 1/4 cup sugar

- 1 1/2 teaspoons salt
- 1 1/4 cups warm water
- 2 tablespoons olive oil
- 1/2 cup dried cranberries
- 1/2 cup chopped walnuts
- 2 teaspoons active dry yeast

Instructions:

1. Add flour, sugar, salt, warm water, olive oil, cranberries, walnuts, and yeast to the bread machine following the manufacturer's guidelines for dough.
2. Choose the dough setting and start the machine.
3. Once the dough is ready, preheat the oven to 375°F (190°C).
4. Shape the dough into a round or oval loaf and place it in a greased loaf pan.
5. Let it rise for 30-45 minutes.
6. Bake for 25-30 minutes or until the top is golden brown.

Nutritional Value (per serving):

- Calories: 250
- Protein: 6g
- Carbohydrates: 45g
- Fat: 6g
- Fiber: 2g

Pesto Swirl Bread Dough

Prep Time: 20 minutes
Cook Time: N/A
Serving Size: 1 loaf

Ingredients:

- 3 cups bread flour
- 1 teaspoon sugar
- 1 1/2 teaspoons salt
- 1 1/4 cups warm water
- 2 tablespoons olive oil
- 1/4 cup pesto sauce
- 2 teaspoons active dry yeast

Instructions:

1. Add flour, sugar, salt, warm water, olive oil, pesto sauce, and yeast to the bread machine following the manufacturer's guidelines for dough.
2. Choose the dough setting and start the machine.
3. Once the dough is ready, preheat the oven to 375°F (190°C).
4. Roll out the dough into a rectangle on a floured surface.
5. Spread a layer of pesto sauce over the dough.
6. Roll the dough into a log and place it in a greased loaf pan.
7. Let it rise for 30-45 minutes.
8. Bake for 25-30 minutes or until the top is golden brown.

Nutritional Value (per serving):

- Calories: 240
- Protein: 6g
- Carbohydrates: 35g
- Fat: 7g
- Fiber: 2.5g

Chocolate Babka Dough

Prep Time: 30 minutes
Cook Time: N/A
Serving Size: 2 babkas

Ingredients:

- 4 cups bread flour
- 1/4 cup sugar
- 1 teaspoon salt
- 1 1/4 cups warm milk
- 1/2 cup unsalted butter, melted
- 2 teaspoons active dry yeast
- 1/2 cup chocolate chips or chunks
- 1/4 cup cocoa powder
- 1/2 cup powdered sugar (for filling)

Instructions:

1. Add flour, sugar, salt, warm milk, melted butter, yeast, chocolate chips, and cocoa powder to the bread machine following the manufacturer's guidelines for dough.
2. Choose the dough setting and start the machine.

3. Once the dough is ready, preheat the oven to 350°F (180°C).
4. Divide the dough into two portions.
5. Roll out each portion into a rectangle.
6. Sprinkle a mixture of powdered sugar and cocoa powder over the dough.
7. Roll the dough into a log and place it in a greased loaf pan.
8. Let it rise for 30-45 minutes.
9. Bake for 30-35 minutes or until the top is golden brown.

Nutritional Value (per serving):

- Calories: 280
- Protein: 5g
- Carbohydrates: 45g
- Fat: 9g
- Fiber: 2.5g

Honey Oat Bread Dough

Prep Time: 15 minutes
Cook Time: N/A
Serving Size: 1 loaf

Ingredients:

- 2 cups bread flour
- 1 cup whole wheat flour
- 1 1/2 teaspoons salt
- 1 1/4 cups warm water
- 1/4 cup honey

- 2 tablespoons olive oil
- 1/2 cup rolled oats
- 2 teaspoons active dry yeast

Instructions:

1. Add bread flour, whole wheat flour, salt, warm water, honey, olive oil, rolled oats, and yeast to the bread machine following the manufacturer's guidelines for dough.
2. Choose the dough setting and start the machine.
3. Once the dough is ready, preheat the oven to 375°F (190°C).
4. Shape the dough into a round or oval loaf and place it in a greased loaf pan.
5. Sprinkle some rolled oats on top.
6. Let it rise for 30 minutes.
7. Bake for 25-30 minutes or until the top is golden brown.

Nutritional Value (per serving):

- Calories: 220
- Protein: 6g
- Carbohydrates: 40g
- Fat: 5g
- Fiber: 4

Chapter Nine

Troubleshooting and Tips

Common Issues

1. **Dense or Heavy Bread:**

   - **Possible Causes:** Insufficient yeast, expired yeast, too much flour, or not enough liquid.

   - **Solution:** Ensure fresh yeast, measure ingredients accurately, and adjust liquid levels according to the specific recipe.

2. **Overly Crusty Bread**

   - **Possible Causes:** Too much flour, too little liquid, or using too much yeast.

   - **Solution:** Adjust the flour-to-liquid ratio and yeast quantity based on the recipe. Experiment with these factors to find the ideal balance.

3. **Bread Collapses or Doesn't Rise**

   - **Possible Causes:** Inactive yeast, expired yeast, or incorrect liquid temperature.

   - **Solution:** Check yeast freshness, use warm (not hot) liquid, and follow the recommended proofing time.

4. **Bread Sticks to the Pan**

   - **Possible Causes:** Insufficient greasing of the pan or not using non-stick spray.

   - **Solution:** Grease the pan thoroughly with butter or non-stick spray before placing the dough.

5. **Uneven Rising**

   - **Possible Causes:** Uneven ingredient distribution in the machine, expired yeast, or old flour.

   - **Solution:** Distribute ingredients evenly and use fresh, quality ingredients.

6. **Excessive Crust Darkness:**

- **Possible Causes:** Too much sugar in the recipe or high oven temperature.
- **Solution:** Reduce sugar amounts and check oven temperature; consider tenting the bread with aluminum foil during baking.

Tips for Success:

1. **Use Fresh Ingredients:**
   - Always use fresh and high-quality ingredients, especially yeast, to ensure optimal bread quality.

2. **Accurate Measurements:**
   - Measure ingredients precisely using the appropriate measuring cups and spoons.

3. **Room Temperature Ingredients:**
   - Allow refrigerated ingredients, like eggs and milk, to reach room temperature before adding them to the bread machine.

4. **Follow Recipe Instructions:**
   - Stick closely to the recipe instructions, including recommended flour and liquid ratios, to achieve the desired results.

5. **Experiment Gradually:**
   - If making adjustments to a recipe, do so gradually, making note of changes and their effects on the final product.

6. **Customize Programs:**
   - Familiarize yourself with your bread machine's features and customize programs based on your preferences and the specific recipe requirements.

7. **Fresh Yeast Test:**
   - Before starting a recipe, conduct a small test with a pinch of yeast in warm water to ensure it bubbles, indicating yeast activity.

8. **Variety in Flours:**

- Experiment with different types of flours, like whole wheat or rye, for diverse and flavorful bread.

9. **Add-Ins and Mix-Ins:**

- Add nuts, seeds, dried fruits, or herbs during the mix-in phase for enhanced flavor and texture.

10. **Maintain the Machine:**

- Regularly clean your bread machine, paying attention to the paddles and baking pan,

7. **Flat Top or Sunken Bread:**

- **Possible Causes:** Too much liquid, over-proofing, or not enough flour.
- **Solution:** Adjust the liquid-to-flour ratio, avoid excessive proofing, and measure flour accurately.

8. **Inconsistent Texture:**

- **Possible Causes:** Uneven ingredient distribution, not following recommended mixing times, or machine issues.
- **Solution:** Distribute ingredients evenly, adhere to mixing times, and ensure the machine is functioning correctly.

9. **Bread Machine Paddle Stuck in Loaf:**

- **Possible Causes:** Paddle not properly secured in the pan or loaf not releasing after baking.
- **Solution:** Ensure the paddle is securely attached before baking and try greasing the paddle before placing it in the pan.

Conclusion

Making homemade bread with your Cuisinart Bread Machine opens you a world of aromatic, fresh, and customized loaves in your own kitchen. Throughout this guidebook, we've covered a wide selection of bread recipes, troubleshooting suggestions, and fundamental recommendations to help you improve your bread-making skills.

This cookbook has something for everyone, from the simplicity of Basic Breads to the indulgence of Sweet Breads, the uniqueness of Specialty Breads, the health-conscious options in Gluten-Free Breads, the artisanal touch of Artisan Breads, and the festive creations in Holiday and Special Occasion Breads.

The inclusion of creative recipes such as Jam and Nut Dispenser, Dough-Only choices, and an assortment of doughs for various baked items demonstrates your Cuisinart Bread Machine's versatility.

As you begin your bread-making journey, don't be afraid to experiment, personalize, and make each recipe your own. Take note of the troubleshooting techniques for overcoming obstacles and adopt the recommended tips for a seamless baking experience.

Baking using a bread machine is about more than simply making loaves; it's about developing a passion for the craft, inhaling the aroma of freshly baked bread, and sharing the joy of homemade deliciousness with family and friends. With each knead and rise, you're establishing memories and traditions that will live long after the final crumb has been relished.

May your kitchen be filled with the pleasant aroma of freshly baked bread, and may your Cuisinart Bread Machine be your faithful friend on this tasty voyage. Happy baking!